PAPUA NEW GUINEA

# Social Science

## Grade 8

# Teacher Resource Book

*Stephen Ranck*

OXFORD

Level 8, 737 Bourke Street, Docklands, Victoria 3008, Australia

Oxford University Press is a department of the University of Oxford. It furthers the University's objective of excellence in research, scholarship, and education by publishing worldwide in

Oxford New York

Auckland Cape Town Dar es Salaam Hong Kong Karachi Kuala Lumpur Madrid Melbourne Mexico City Nairobi New Delhi Shanghai Taipei Toronto

With offices in

Argentina Austria Brazil Chile Czech Republic France Greece Guatemala Hungary Italy Japan Poland Portugal Singapore South Korea Switzerland Thailand Turkey Ukraine Vietnam



First published 2008
Reprinted 2008, 2009, 2010, 2014, 2023 (D)



ISBN 978 0 19 555514 1
Typeset by Cathy Rose
Printed and bound in Australia by Ligare Book Printers Pty Ltd

# Contents


| | | |
|---|---|---|
| **Overview** | | **1** |
| Social Science for Grade 8 | | 1 |
| Using the Student Book | | 2 |
| Using the Teacher Resource Book | | 3 |
| Learning Outcomes | | 5 |
| Guide to the Syllabus | | 6 |
| **Introduction** | | **7** |
| **Strand 1:** | **Environment and Resources** | **9** |
| About this strand | | |
| **Sub-strand** | **People and Environment** | |
| 8.1.1 | The physical and human environment | 10 |
| Main ideas | | 10 |
| Possible assessment tasks | | 11 |
| Teacher information | | 12 |
| 8.1.2 | How physical environments influence human settlement patterns in the world | 20 |
| 8.1.3 | The impact of resource use on the world's physical environments and human settlement patterns | 20 |
| 8.1.4 | International examples of sustainable practices to the natural environment and possible solutions to problems | 20 |
| Main ideas | | 20 |
| Possible assessment tasks | | 22 |
| Teacher information | | 23 |
| 8.1.5 | The causes and effects of hazardous natural events in other parts of the world and how people respond to them | 30 |
| Main ideas | | 30 |
| Possible assessment tasks | | 33 |
| Teacher information | | 34 |

**Strand 2** **Organisation** **35**

About this strand

**Sub-strand:** **Social and Economic Organisation**

8.2.1 The form and origin of contemporary, traditional and constitutional government in other parts of the world 36

8.2.2 Conditions that have led to the present day international forms of trade and government 36

8.2.3 Changes to trade and government that would lead to social and economic development at international level 36

Main ideas 36

Possible assessment tasks 37

Teacher information 39

**Strand 3** **Culture** **50**

About this strand

**Sub-strand:** **Cultural Expression**

8.3.1 Comparing elements of other national cultures with our own 51

8.3.2 Identifying key elements that shape international culture 51

8.3.3 Participating in international culture 51

Main ideas 51

Possible assessment tasks 52

Teacher Information 55

**Strand 4** **Integrating Projects** **67**

About this strand

**Sub-strand:** **Societies and Communities**

8.4.1 Using the social science process to describe another nation and propose ways for Papua New Guinea to contribute more to the region 67

8.4.2 Using the social science process to describe an international society and propose ways for Papua New Guinea to be more involved in international affairs 67

Main ideas 67

Possible assessment tasks 70

Teacher Information 70

**Glossary** **74**

# Overview

## Social Science for Grade 8

Social Science was introduced to students in Grade 6, when they began looking at their own communities. The Grade 7 text expanded coverage to the national level and to the regions around Papua New Guinea. Grade 8 explores the world's environment, settlements, population, history, governments, trade and culture. This Teacher Resource Book supports the student text with explanatory and supplementary material. It also will help guide you on how to use resources to keep material fresh and current.

You will be able to link much of the Grade 8 content back to the students' studies in Grades 6 and 7. Students can compare what they have learned about their local, national and regional areas with other parts of the world. You should also ensure that students continue to use all the basic concepts learned in the earlier years.

The Grade 8 Student Book gives students a taste of what the world offers. The text provides a starting point and the teacher can build on material covered in previous years. You can explore connections with the students, and develop themes to show how the environment, settlement, government and other parts of culture are connected. You will be able to give students a base for further understanding as they continue to mature, and allow them to explore areas of special interest. You can use Papua New Guinea as a basis for comparisons, and ask students how the many concepts they have studied apply to the larger world. Roles, responsibilities, bias, rights, and rituals are all elements that students can search for in many of the studies.

The world is full of many different values and attitudes. You and your students may agree with some and disagree with others. The key is to teach respect for the way different people and places have developed. Every culture will have its good and bad parts. No culture is completely free of crime, corruption or conflict.

Much of your current information will come from newspapers, radio and other popular sources. Be sure that students understand how selective much of this information is. Always have them search for bias and 'the other side of the story'. You will need to carefully guide class research to balance bias and prejudice that may be evident in news sources. Some students may have access to the Internet, which offers a wealth of information. But remember that many sites remain unchecked and may contain false, misleading or biased information.

Another way of researching or comparing different places in the world is through photo interpretation. Students can collect news and magazine photos on different themes, and use them to compare and contrast different situations in the world. Again, it is important to ask, 'What is missing?' What is not shown is sometimes just as important as what is shown.

## Using the Student Book

### Key features

The Grade 8 Student Book consists of an introduction and four chapters. Each chapter follows the syllabus, and covers one strand and one sub-strand. Some of the sub-strands have been divided into sections to make it easier for the students and teacher to follow. The Teacher Resource Book also provides more detailed information on some of the more complex areas of the syllabus.

**Overview:** Please note that the Grade 8 syllabus covers a lot of content. Teachers will have to judge the levels that students can achieve. Different locations will have different resources and students will have very different interests about the Earth, and its many social, political, cultural and economic systems. Encourage students to find and select areas that really interest them. Everyone can find something of interest with the whole world to choose from. Be sure students share their different studies. This will add to everyone's knowledge.

Encourage your students to use whatever resources are available. Getting current information is very important as the world is constantly changing. The text can provide a foundation, teaching about processes and the past. This guide will help teachers and students find ways to get information on the present. Students can then consider what may happen in the future.

**The introduction** provides a quick review of some important concepts that students have studied in the previous two years. These concepts should be used across the four chapters, or strands, that follow.

**Chapter 1** looks at physical and human interactions on the Earth. It follows the same pattern as the first two years. The first chapter in Grades 6 and 7 ended with a study of natural hazards. In Grade 8, students look at the mix of human and natural hazards. The chapter closes with an exploration of the important issue of global warming, or climate change, as a major emerging hazard.

**Chapter 2** covers systems of government and offers an overview of the history of world governments and international trade. It closes with a look at how much progress has been made in stopping (or abolishing) the slave trade around the world. The abolition of legal slavery is a great international achievement.

**Chapter 3** explores culture and cultural expression. It uses a collection of photographs and images to provide a wide-ranging visual base for discussions about culture around the world. It also explores culture on each continent and global cultural concepts. Materials from Strands 2 and 3 can be used in discussions on globalisation. The chapter looks at different ways of studying culture through ideas, sayings, myths and stories. It ends with a discussion on the destruction and preservation of culture. Students can further explore all of these aspects of culture around the world.

**Chapter 4** challenges students to do project work about some part or parts of the world. The key here is to maintain balance and consider all sides of an argument or problem. Encourage your students to find an integrating project that they are really interested in doing. The more interest they have, the better they will do. In many parts of Papua New Guinea, students will be challenged to find information about distant parts of the world. The integrating projects will need imagination and resourcefulness to find and use available information.

The **glossary** from the Student Book is repeated on page 74–76 of the Teacher Resource Book for easy reference.

## Using the Teacher Resource Book

This Teacher Resource Book provides a guide to teaching Social Science for Grade 8.

### Key features

Students will be pursuing information about distant places in the world. Much of this information will carry attitudes and values. There will be prejudice and bias in radio and newspaper reports and other current information. They may only give a small amount of information about a place. Papua New Guineans who travel overseas find the same applies to Papua New Guinea. The further from home, the less people know about a place. And what they do know is often biased and unbalanced. The teacher's task is to help students achieve balance.

Compare and discuss all the available information as individuals and a class. Have the class examine the attitudes and values that they find in the different materials. As students consider political, economic and government issues, they will come across information that will need balance and discussion.

Where students are interviewing people to gain information, it is a good idea to be sure this is done in groups or with adult supervision. There may be times when it is appropriate for groups of males to interview males and females to interview females.

We continue to follow a simplified social science process: SEE – UNDERSTAND – ACT. These are the three steps for students to follow in their social science studies. The second step could also be called CONSIDER, EVALUATE, or APPRAISE. (The syllabus uses 'judge', however this could confuse students.)

The three-step process includes the following skills:

- SEE: form questions, prepare a study, gather information
- UNDERSTAND: analyse and evaluate the information, make conclusions (but understand that more information later may change your conclusions)
- ACT: present the information or take action (and then consider the results again).

## How to use it

When you receive this book you need to:

- review it to get an idea of the information it contains and its organisation
- consider how you can most fully involve students
- read it carefully to see how you can apply it and the Student Book to the world, national and regional situation in terms of the strands, sub-strands, processes, elaborations and learning outcomes
- map out your teaching and learning strategies
- identify specific projects that your students could undertake based on the learning outcomes, and check what your students are interested in (but note that different students or groups of students may have interest in very different projects that may be developed over time)
- consider how to use the information to develop your own programs and units of work.

## Structure

This Teacher Resource Book is structured in the following way:

- Each chapter covers one syllabus strand (Environment and Resources, Organisation, Culture, Integrating Projects). Details of the syllabus are shown in the table, 'Guide to the Syllabus and the Organisation of the Teacher Resource Book'. The table is located in the Learning Outcomes section that follows. You can use this table to help plan the various units of work. The learning outcomes are broad and can be achieved in many different ways. Your approach will depend on available resources and expertise.
- In Grade 8, these strands focus on the world and include the four major oceans (Pacific, Atlantic, Arctic, Indian), and the seven continents (Africa, Antarctica, Asia, Australia, Europe, North America, South America).
- There is an introduction to each chapter that names the strand and sub-strand, with a brief overview of the material that follows.
- Each chapter has the information organised in sections based on the learning outcomes. Sometimes these sections are presented separately. Sometimes they are combined. In both cases, the material in each section is divided into:  
  Main ideas  
  Example of elaborating the learning outcome  
  Possible assessment tasks  
  Teacher information (this material adds to the main ideas)

The Student Book starts with an introduction. This provides an important base for the material to follow. It is covered in this book, with a shorter piece of information.

## Learning Outcomes

This Teacher Resource Book follows the curriculum. The Grade 8 syllabus is divided into four strands. Each strand in this syllabus has one sub-strand. Each sub-strand has a number of learning outcomes. The learning outcomes have been divided into sections. Each section is listed as the focus for that learning outcome.

The learning outcomes describe what a student should be able to do after finishing a particular part of the curriculum. In Grade 8, the focus is on the world beyond Papua New Guinea and its region. This is an enormous area to cover so much of it will be a relatively brief summary. With three hours of class time a week, you will have to decide how quickly to move through the course.

To study the world, you will need to look for a wide range of materials and areas to compare. Students can use Papua New Guinea as a base for comparison with other places and events in the world. The choices are almost unlimited.

If there is one key theme or idea that you can follow through all four chapters of Grade 8, it is this: there is just one world. Everyone is part of that world. All parts of the planet Earth are interconnected including oceans, continents, islands, the atmosphere and the people too. Human activities from trade to manufacturing to warfare can impact and change the Earth. The Earth also changes naturally. Human cultures adapt to change or suffer by failing to adapt.

## Guide to the Syllabus

This table outlines the content against the syllabus. The learning focus is added to help you with learning outcomes. The title of each section is regarded as the focus for the learning outcome.

| Chapter | Strand | Sub-strand | Section or Learning Focus | Learning Outcomes |
|---|---|---|---|---|
| Introduction | Overview to Social Science | Social Science | Overview | Students start to think about the entire world and how much they might learn by applying basic social science concepts to their studies |
| 1 | Environment and Resources | People and Environment | The physical and human environment | 8.1.1 Students are able to compare and contrast the main physical environments of the world and describe the factors and processes that have formed them |
| 1 | Environment and Resources | People and Environment | Adapting to the physical environment | 8.1.2 Students are able to analyse how physical environments influence human settlement patterns in the world |
| 1 | Environment and Resources | People and Environment | Changing the physical environment | 8.1.3 Students are able to evaluate the impact of resource use on the world's physical environments and human settlement patterns |
| 1 | Environment and Resources | People and Environment | Working to sustain the physical environment | 8.1.4 Students are able to identify international examples of sustainable practices in the natural environment and propose possible solutions to problems |
| 1 | Environment and Resources | People and Environment | Natural hazards, combining human and natural hazards and the environment | 8.1.5 Students are able to identify and describe the causes and effects of hazardous natural events in other parts of the world and how people respond to them |
| 2 | Organisation | Social and Economic Organisation | Governments past and present around the world | 8.2.1 Students are able to identify and describe the form and origin of contemporary, traditional and constitutional government in other parts of the world |
| 2 | Organisation | Social and Economic Organisation | Resources past and present around the world | 8.2.2 Students are able to outline conditions that have led to the present day international forms of trade and government |
| 2 | Organisation | Social and Economic Organisation | Overview for action to contribute to development | 8.2.3 Students are able to suggest changes to trade and government that would lead to social and economic development at the international level |
| 3 | Culture | Cultural Expression | Cultural comparisons | 8.3.1 Students are able to compare elements of other national cultures with our own |
| 3 | Culture | Cultural Expression | Many ways to view culture | 8.3.2 Students are able to identify key elements that shape international culture |
| 3 | Culture | Cultural Expression | Student-centred culture studies | 8.3.3 Students are able to participate in international culture |
| 4 | Integrating Projects | Societies and Communities | Allowing students to choose an area of interest for an integrating project | 8.4.1 Students are able to use the social science process to describe another nation and propose ways for Papua New Guinea to contribute more to the region |
| 4 | Integrating Projects | Societies and Communities | Allowing students to choose an area of interest for an integrating project that includes an international society | 8.4.2 Students are able to use the social science process to describe an international society and to propose ways for Papua New Guinea to be more involved in international affairs |
| 5 | Appendices | Glossary | | |

# Introduction

The introduction in the Student Book provides an overview to the studies to follow. It is important that students have some idea of where they are going. The world is a big place. They will be gaining an understanding about some of the ways in which the world works.

To introduce the world, or the planet Earth, have students make a list with the title 'Places that I know little or nothing about'. Have them keep this list in a safe place or keep it for them. Near the end of the course, the students can re-visit the list. They should now have a better idea of the variety in the world and the ways that our planet functions.

In Grades 6 and 7, students started working with some social science concepts. It is important to review and continue using these concepts in Grade 8. The following table will help you. At the beginning and end of each chapter or section, you can review these concepts with the students. This can serve to confirm learning and generate further discussion.

| | |
|---|---|
| Values | What are values? What values will be important in studying the world? How do you think values change around the world? Can you think of values that people may share around the world? |
| Attitudes | What are attitudes? What attitudes do you have about other parts of the world? Do you care about other parts of the world? What type of an attitude is that? |
| Prejudice | What is prejudice? What prejudices do you think you will find around the world? What prejudices do you have about other parts of the world? |
| Bias | What is bias? Can you find any examples of bias in the news about the world? Have you heard biased statements about other places or other people in the world? |
| Roles | What are roles? How many roles can you think of that are found around the world? How different are they from roles in Papua New Guinea? |
| Responsibilities | What are responsibilities? What do you think world responsibilities are? What do you think international responsibilities are? |
| Rights | What are rights? What rights do people have around the world? Are there international rights? How can countries agree on rights? |
| Sustainability | What is sustainability? |
| Behaviour | What is behaviour? |
| Good behaviour (or positive behaviour) | What is good behaviour (or positive behaviour)? |
| Bad behaviour (or negative behaviour) | What is bad behaviour (or negative behaviour)? |
| Adaptation (and failure to adapt) | What is adaptation (and failure to adapt)? |
| The social science process | What is the social science process? |
| Other concepts that you remember | What are other concepts that you remember? |

These questions will help students to explore ideas about the world. The key for teachers is to ensure respect and balance in their answers, which may vary widely. The aim should be to remove bias and prejudice.

Students will find many news reports about distant parts of the world. It is important that they understand the articles are not representative, and may be sensational. For example here are two different headlines:

- *Frog juice proves a hit in Peru* (*Post Courier*, Monday 7 May 2007): a close reading of the article shows that in the city of Lima, Peru, perhaps a couple of hundred people drink liquidised frogs. It tells the reader very little about Peru. Studying an atlas would show that Lima is the capital of Peru and has a population of millions of people. So the bias in the article is in the headline. The frog juice is a hit with a few hundred people out of millions. This type of article can be reviewed using the concepts in the previous table. This is the type of article that is often found about Papua New Guinea in the world press.
- *Judge forces shoplifters to wear 'I am a thief' sign* (*The National*, Tuesday 8 May 2007): this article is about a judge who has made thieves stand outside the store they stole from with signs around their necks, in the United States of America. It looks at a very odd or unusual occurrence. This is a nation of 250 million people. How much does it really tell the reader about the American justice system?

Have students look for articles that provide unusual or sensational news. Discuss them in class to see what they actually do and do not teach about the world. You can also ask students why such articles are popular.

Students can use pictures in the text and pictures they find from other sources to explore, review and analyse different places, concepts and activities around the world. From the start, try using pictures to challenge students to analyse what is happening. For example, find some pictures of a busy city or of a rural area in the weekend newspapers or magazines. Ask the students, 'Think of what you have learned so far about social science. Look at the following pictures. What can you tell about them? What seems similar to you and what seems different? Can you tell where they come from?'

Divide the class into two teams or groups. Each team takes one picture to see how many concepts in the table apply to the picture. Ask each team, 'How does the concept apply to the picture?' For example, how does the concept of 'values' apply to a picture of a city? Discuss the pictures and concepts with both groups. What concepts and ideas can you add to their original lists?

STRAND 1

# Environment and Resources

## About this strand

The Environment and Resources strand has one sub-strand, People and Environment. The strand and sub-strand cover a very wide range of topics. You will be able to find supporting material in newspapers, books, magazines and radio programs. This is a good opportunity to challenge students to find more information on the different sections listed below. Information about people and the environment around the world will impact students for all their lives.

This sub-strand is divided into five sections:

- The physical and human environment
- Adapting to the physical environment
- Changing the physical environment
- Working to sustain the physical environment
- Natural hazards and the environment.

There is a large amount of work to cover in these five sections. You can choose different areas to focus on. This is a changing topic. Examples of major areas of change include:

- climate change or global warming
- diseases such as bird flu
- pollution
- resource use (especially essentials like energy and water)
- population growth
- migration and refugees
- armed conflict
- technology (especially risks like access to nuclear weapons)
- democracy, governance and fighting corruption.

Teaching resources will vary depending on where the school is located. All areas will have some resources available. It is up to the teacher to inspire students to search out resources. This will greatly help them add more meaning to the studies. Look for comparisons and contrasts in human interaction with the environment around the world.

The five People and the Environment learning outcomes are covered in three sections in the material that follows. An 'Example of elaborating a learning outcome' is given for each section.

# 8.1.1 The physical and human environment

## Main ideas

This section introduces many concepts. It provides students with an overview of the physical world. Students will need to use an atlas when available for detailed information. The physical map of the world on the inside front cover shows some features of the physical world, but not in great detail. The map only shows the surface of the world. Students will consider the atmosphere and have been introduced to sub-surface tectonic plate movement in previous years. Major concepts include the physical world (our planet, Earth) and some of its major features; mapping the world and how to map a globe; describing locations on Earth; and the biosphere (that part of the Earth that supports life). Note that in this section, the syllabus only covers some of the major features of the biosphere. For example, swamps are not covered. Some students might want to touch on this in their integrating projects and there is no reason to discourage them if resources are available. The same principles of interaction, human adaptation and other concepts will apply.

### Example of elaborating a learning outcome

**Strand:** Environment and Resources

**Sub-strand:** People and Environment

**Focus:** The physical and human environment

**Learning outcome 8.1.1:** Students are able to compare and contrast the main physical environments of the world and describe the factors and processes that have formed them.

Social Science is to be timetabled for 180 minutes a week in all Upper Primary Schools. Generally this will allow for a one-hour lesson three times a week. In some instances, depending on scheduling flexibility, there may be scope for a one-hour lesson on one day and a two-hour lesson another day. There are numerous ways to elaborate the material. In Grade 8, the major issue for teachers will be the amount of time needed to complete the syllabus. Elaborations may only be one or two hours given the large amount of material to be covered. In some instances, they may be less than an hour where students have 15 to 30 minutes to carry on with a topic. This is possible where they have sought out further information. The following is a possible elaboration for one week:

| Monday | Wednesday |
|---|---|
| *Second half-hour of class*<br>Discuss with the class the different types of climate zones that exist in the world. Then have them choose one feature (such as rivers, mountains, forests, islands, etc.) and explore how these are different in different climate zones. (This could extend to human populations and adaptations to different features and zones.) | *First half-hour of the class*<br>Have the class groups report on their findings. For example, what differences have they found in islands in different climate zones? How do mountains change in different climate zones? What information have students been able to gather and evaluate? |

### Key words

the physical world, planet Earth, mapping, the Poles, hemispheres, latitude, longitude, prime meridian, equator, the Earth's surface, atmosphere, climate zones, oceans, the water cycle, continents, islands, mountains, rivers, forests, biosphere



**Possible assessment tasks**

The following tasks can be done on paper or as an oral report. They can be done for individual or group assessment:

1 Choose any continent and choose two physical features like mountains and rivers, or grasslands and forest. Describe these features and see what details you can find out about them. Then compare them with the same features in Papua New Guinea or on New Guinea Island.

2 Assign students to report on ways to make a flat map of the Earth. How does it change from a globe or sphere? See if they can determine the scale if they know that the equator is 40 000 kilometres in length. They may need assistance from the maths teacher for this.

3 Compare two different climate zones in the world. Give reasons for the differences. Explain the advantages and disadvantages of each area (what is good about that type of climate zone and what is bad about that type of climate zone).

4 Compare the physical environments of two continents. Depending on how many students are in the class, every continent can be compared at least once with another continent.

5 Collect more information about the four major oceans. Make comparisons if resources are available.

6 See what information students can find on any of the world's longest rivers. How are these rivers different from the Sepik, Fly or Musa in Papua New Guinea?

7 See what information students can find on any of the world's major mountains. How different are these mountains from the Owen Stanley Range, or the Highlands or the mountains of Goodenough Island in Papua New Guinea?

8 Compare the features of the world's ten largest islands. What other information can students find out about these ten islands?

9 Make posters about the grasslands of Africa, North America and South America (or places where this information is available to students).

10 Write a song to sing to the class that lists all seven continents and some of the major physical features in each continent.

# Teacher information

## The physical world

The physical world is the basis for all life. The basic surface features of the physical world are land and water. Another vital feature is the atmosphere. A small part of the atmosphere consists of the air we breathe. A larger part of the atmosphere is responsible for climate and weather as it interacts with the physical world.

Human beings interact with the physical world. The sections and chapters after this first section all deal with human actions. All human actions interact with the physical world. People often forget or ignore this. And different cultures treat the physical world differently. These are themes that students can explore in their studies. At any point in the text they should be able to return to the first section of Chapter 1 and observe the interconnections between the study material and the physical world.

### Planet Earth and other planets

We live on a planet. Planets are round. They can be called globes or spheres. You can use a ball or any round fruit to explain some of the features of the Earth to students. You can also have students use a globe or a ball or any round fruit to see some of the problems in mapping the surface of the Earth.

The Earth is one of eight planets in our solar system. Planet Earth and the other planets in our solar system orbit (or go around) the sun. There are also many other items that orbit around the sun. It takes the Earth 365 and a quarter days to orbit the sun. That is why our year is 365 days long for three years and then 366 days every fourth year (or leap year). Sometimes the Earth is a little closer or further from the sun. This does not make a big difference. Our planet is about 150 million kilometres away from the sun on average.

It is important for students to understand the importance of Earth's environment compared with other planets. If we were further away from the sun, it could be too cold for life. Jupiter and the planets beyond are far from the sun. It is very cold on these planets. Mars is cold too, but maybe it had a better environment a long time ago. Venus and Mercury are very hot, because they are closer to the sun than the Earth, and much too hot for almost all of our environments.

Earth is part of the universe. Science dates the Earth at about four and a half billion years old. Earth is subject to physical forces from the sun and moon. The tides, climates and seasons are all impacted by these forces.

The Earth also rotates on its axis. It completes a full rotation (or spins around in a circle) every 24 hours as it travels around the sun. The Earth rotates on its axis every 24 hours as it travels around the sun. This gives us day and night. The orbit and rotation of the Earth on an angled axis give us seasons.

The seasons in the temperate zones of the Earth change markedly because of the angle of the Earth's axis. As the Earth goes around the sun, the Northern Hemisphere is closer to the sun for half the year. It is closest in June, the Northern Hemisphere summer. The Southern Hemisphere gets closer to the sun during the other half of the year. It is closest in December, the Southern Hemisphere summer. The change from warmer to colder to warmer to colder makes the seasons year after year.

Another main change is the length of daylight. In temperate and Arctic zones of the Earth, the changes can be many hours more or less of daylight depending on the season (more daylight in the summer and much less daylight in the winter). At the Poles, there is constant daylight at the peak of the summer season and complete darkness day after day at the peak of winter.

People in Papua New Guinea are very close to the Equator. They do not notice much change because they are in the tropics. For example, in Port Moresby there is about half an hour more daylight in December-January (the Southern Hemisphere summer) than in June-July (the Southern Hemisphere winter).

The Earth rotates toward the east. You can use a globe or sphere to show this to students. The new day could start in any place but people decided to start it in the Pacific Ocean and they created an imaginary line, or starting point, called the International Dateline. This point is convenient because it is far from most of the world's population.

### Environments on other planets

Scientists have been searching to see if the environment on other planets could support life. Astronomers are scientists who study outer space. A famous astronomer thought he saw channels on Mars many years ago. Some people thought these were channels made by some type of life. With better telescopes, people came to see that there was no sign of life on Mars. Later, rockets have placed mechanical probes on Mars. Still there is no firm evidence of life.

Scientists also think there might be life on one of Jupiter's moons and are trying to explore this. They are also trying to listen for signs of intelligent life from beyond our solar system, using radio telescopes. Some astronomers are finding gigantic planets that orbit other stars. Studies continue. No one has found life or intelligent life anywhere but Earth.

You can ask students the following questions in class:

- What environment is needed to support life?
- Why are people interested in looking for life on other planets?
- What values or attitudes influence the search for life away from Earth?
- Is the Earth's environment very special to be able to support life or is the Earth's environment not so special? Could there be many other places like it in the universe?

## Mapping the world

Mapping the world is actually very difficult. It has taken people a long time to make accurate maps. The first main problem was how to map a globe on a flat piece of paper. This challenged mapmakers for hundreds of years. Having students trying to do this will show many of the problems.

Students can work by themselves or in a small group. First find a sphere. Have them find a range of spheres; for example, an orange, a pomelo or maybe a round ball like a soccer ball. Their task is to put a map of the world on a sphere. Just try to label the continents and the Pacific and Atlantic oceans. If they use an orange, they could draw or paint on the skin. If they use a ball, they will need to cut out paper labels and stick them on. If they use an orange, have them try to make a flat map from the skin. They should peel it off carefully and see what happens when they flatten it. What is the problem? If they use a ball, what happens when they try to stick flat paper onto the curved surface?

Discuss the problems they find in class, and how there is distortion when we try to make a flat map of the curved Earth.

Changing curved surfaces to flat surfaces will change the scales in different parts of the map. It also creates illusions. The best world map is a globe. But carrying around a globe is not very practical. Flat maps are much more practical. You can discuss with students how difficult it would be to map some places without satellites or aerial images.

## Describing locations on Earth

The simplest way to describe locations on Earth is to divide the world into hemispheres. We use the equator to divide the world into the Northern Hemisphere and the Southern Hemisphere. The equator is an imaginary line that runs around the world. It is 40 000 kilometres long. Remember that the Earth is spinning on its axis at a 23.5-degree angle to the sun. At one end of the axis is the North Pole. At the other end of the axis is the South Pole. Places on Earth can be located on the Northern or Southern Hemispheres. Note that some countries will be in both hemispheres. Refer to the diagrams in the Student Book.

### A review of maps

Remember, maps are a type of picture. The simplest map is a sketch that can be made on the ground, on the blackboard or on paper. Review the three important features of maps with your students.

- **Orientation:** the normal rule or practice is to orient a map to the north when it is drawn. When you hold the map, or look at one of the maps in the book, north should be at the top of the page. This is the same with a globe. It will have the North Pole at the top (at an angle of 23.5 degrees to show how the Earth is tilted toward the sun). Orientation is a convention. We could agree that all maps have south at the top. It is just that the first mapmakers in Europe decided on north. The cardinal points are north, south, east and west. We use these points with latitude and longitude to describe locations on Earth.
- **Scale:** a scale is a type of ratio. Students will now have two years of experience with this. If they are still confused, have them review ratios with their maths teacher and in maths studies. The scale used to show large parts of the world on a map will be very small. It may be one to a million (1:1 000 000). A map of the whole world represents 40 000 kilometres from one end of the equator to the other. In a large atlas, the scale for this may be around one to 100 million (1:100 000 000). In a small atlas, the scale may be at one to 200 million (1:200 000 000) or more. A scale of 1 to 100 million means that for every centimetre on the map, there are 100 million centimetres on the ground. A hundred million centimetres is the same as 1 000 kilometres. So two places on that map that are 40 centimetres apart are 40 000 kilometres apart on the ground. (That is the length of the equator.)
- **Key:** the key to a map tells you what features are on it. It may identify physical features, such as forests, mountains, rivers and oceans. It can also give symbols for human features including political boundaries.

### Latitude, longitude, and prime meridian

Students were introduced to latitude and longitude in Grade 7. Latitude and longitude are used to determine locations anywhere in the world. Teachers can review them in Grade 8. It is best to use a globe if one is available, or an atlas. Having students make their own simple globes of the Earth using balls or fruit will quickly help them grasp these concepts.

Latitude and longitude are lines on the map. They look like a grid on the map but they look different on a globe.

Lines of latitude run east and west. Lines of longitude run north and south. Latitudes lines run parallel to the equator and each other. (Sometimes they are called 'parallels'.) They represent degrees of distance north and south of the equator. They start at the equator at zero degrees. Lines of latitude become shorter in distance as they move further away from the equator.

Lines of longitude run from the North Pole to the South Pole. Again they are measured in degrees around the Earth. They do not run parallel to each other. The first one is at zero degrees. It goes through Greenwich, England. It is also called the Prime Meridian. Lines of longitude then move east and west until they reach 180 degrees, which is the other side of the world. They are all the same length, about 20 000 kilometres.

The prime meridian is used as a base for time. In the old days of sailing ships, a captain needed to know Greenwich time and local time to help tell him what longitude he was at. Ships needed very accurate clocks or chronometers. Now people use satellite systems for navigation.

Remember that Papua New Guinea's northern sea border starts on the equator at 0 degrees and extends 12 degrees of latitude to the south. Port Moresby is about 147 degrees east of Greenwich and nine degrees south of the equator.

## The atmosphere

The air we breathe, the weather and the climates all come from the atmosphere. Students should understand that only a small part of the atmosphere has enough oxygen for humans to survive. The other parts are important. They protect us from too much sunlight. They provide the basis for climate and for weather.

The atmosphere interacts with the physical surface of the Earth. The Earth's rotation and orbit around the sun create changes to the atmosphere. Students need to understand that all these functions on Earth are interconnected.

The atmosphere that supports life (people, animals, plants) is only a few kilometres deep. The atmosphere gets thinner and thinner as you go higher. At sea level, there is plenty of oxygen to breathe. There is less oxygen with increasing elevation. After the first 3 000 metres, or three kilometres, there is little human settlement. Few people or animals can survive at 4 000 metres or higher.

The tallest mountains on Earth rise so high that there is not enough oxygen in that part of the atmosphere for people to live there. The climate on mountaintops is also cold and difficult for humans. Mt Everest is the tallest mountain above sea level on Earth. It is 8 848 metres tall. No one can live at that altitude for more than a very short time. Every year, people pay guides to help them get to the top of Mt Everest. People can pay as much as 100 000 kina. Every year, some of these people die. Most must carry oxygen with them. No one stays for more than 20 to 30 minutes at the top. It is too cold and there is not enough oxygen to breathe. Like people, animals and vegetation keep to lower elevations or altitudes where there is more oxygen in the atmosphere.

## Climate zones

The Earth can be divided into climate zones. The climate zones exist for a number of reasons. One important reason is the world wind system. It is called the general circulation of the atmosphere. This system carries warm and cold air long distances around the world. The winds circulate warm and cold air and this has a major impact on the climate zones.

Other important reasons why we have climate zones are the rotation of the Earth on its axis and the orbit of the Earth around the sun. Remember too that the atmosphere interacts with the oceans and the land. Mountains can change climates by blocking or capturing moist air in the atmosphere.

There are four major climate zones. Note also that climates vary around the world with altitude and other special conditions. The four major zones are:

- the wet and warm tropical (or equatorial) zone around the equator
- the dryer subtropical zones where temperatures can vary and deserts can occur
- the temperate zones which have a mild climate and four seasons – spring, summer, autumn and winter
- the cold polar zones at the highest latitudes, which are covered with snow and ice.

Refer to the diagram in the Student Book.

Winds around the world are created by the differences between hot and cold air. The heat rises around the equator. It cools and sinks about 30 degrees to north and south of the equator. This is repeated until you reach the north and south poles. These are the coldest places on Earth.

Students can watch hot air rise from a fire. If they live near mountains, they can feel cold air sink down from the mountains at night. Those same principles make wind around the world. The winds would go from the equator to the south and the north if the Earth did not rotate. The Earth's rotation makes winds generally blow from the east to the west in the Northern Hemisphere and from west to east in the Southern Hemisphere.

Students can play a game in teams using the maps. One team names a month and a place in the temperate zone. The other team tells what season it is. For example, July in Sydney, Australia, is winter; July in New York, United States of America, is summer; April in Hamburg, Germany, is spring; April in Santiago, Chile, is autumn. This table shows the temperate seasons around the world.

| **Season by month in the Northern Hemisphere** | | | |
|---|---|---|---|
| January | Winter | July | Summer |
| February | Winter | August | Summer |
| March | Spring | September | Autumn |
| April | Spring | October | Autumn |
| May | Spring | November | Autumn |
| June | Summer | December | Winter |

Another type of season is the monsoon. The word 'monsoon' comes from Arabic and it means 'season'. This change in climate is caused by changes in heating and cooling of the oceans and continents. The result is winds that change direction to create different seasons. India and South East Asia have monsoons. The summer monsoon brings heavy rainfall to India. The wind blows south-westerly across the Indian Ocean. The winter monsoon is generally dry. It blows north-easterly across the Indian Ocean. Students can investigate how monsoons impact Papua New Guinea and compare this with other places.

There is tropical weather and tropical climate around the equator (check that students remember the difference between 'weather' and 'climate'). There is often little wind because the hot air is rising. It cools and falls a long way away. This made it hard for sailing ships in the old days. At sea, the sailors called tropical areas 'the doldrums'. Ships could be stuck if all they had was sails for power, but no wind to drive them. How is the term 'the doldrums' used today? Challenge students to find out what it has come to mean. They could also find examples of how the words 'tropical' and 'equatorial' are used. 'Tropical', 'equatorial' and 'the doldrums' all describe parts of the same place. But the values behind these words and the way they are used can be very different. Have students discuss this in class.

## Oceans

Oceans take up about three quarters, or 75 per cent, of the Earth's surface. Water is the basis of life, as we know it. The oceans are made up of different layers with different pressures and temperatures. They provide the base for the water cycle. The sun's rays heat and evaporate water. This forms clouds. The clouds release the water. This falls back on the land or sea. Even when it falls back on land, much of it eventually washes to the sea. The water cycle is essential for life on the land.

The oceans are often called 'heat sinks'. This means they hold and move heat. The oceans receive about 66 per cent of all the solar heat that reaches the Earth.

Changes in the oceans make changes to climate. A good example of the oceans and their impact on both climate and weather is the el niño effect. This is a warming of waters in the Pacific Ocean off the coast of Peru. It can result in drought in places as far away as Australia and Papua New Guinea. And it can result in extra rainfall with floods in other places like the coast of Ecuador or Christmas Island, Kiribati.

Students may read or hear about the el niño effect (now sometimes called the southern oscillation index). El niño (pronounced 'ninyo') is Spanish. It means 'a male child'. In this case, it means the Christ child. Peruvian fishermen used the term because an el niño effect usually started near Christmas. The warmer water brought them many more fish. The fisherman considered the fish a Christmas gift. Other places people did not think that drought or flood was a gift! You can discuss this example with students and talk about how different cultures interpret parts of the physical world.

## Continents

The seven continents are major landmasses – Africa, Antarctica, Asia, Australia, Europe, North America and South America. In some places in the world, people combine the Americas into one continent but we refer to seven continents in this course.

The ancient Greeks were the first to define the continents. The Aegean Sea was the centre of the world for them. Have students find Greece and the Aegean Sea on a map. The ancient Greeks started with two continents: Europe to the west of them and Asia to the east. People still talk about the East when they mean Asia. And people still talk and write about the West. Ask students, 'Who is the West now?' and discuss in class.

Later, the Greeks decided that there was a third continent. They named it Africa. For thousands of years, Europeans only knew of these three continents.

Ask students why the ancient Greeks put themselves at the centre of the continents. Where is Greece today? Where is the centre of the world now? Finally, ask the students what values and attitudes terms like East and West carry?

## Islands

Islands are smaller land areas than continents. The Student Book lists the ten largest islands in the world. This is just one approach to islands and the world. It is up to the teacher to extend students' thinking. For example, you can ask the students questions such as:

- What settlements can you find on these islands?
- How large do you think the populations are for these islands?
- What hazards might the people on them face?

Students should also be asked to decide what important islands are not in the list of the ten largest islands. This should start them thinking what makes this feature important? You can do this same type of exercise with mountains, forests and other physical features.

## Mountains

Mountains are where the land rises up steeply to over 300 metres. Papua New Guinea and some other parts of the world are very mountainous. Tectonic plates coming together push land upwards. The more recently created mountains are steep and sharply pointed. Older mountain ranges like the Snowy Mountains in Australia or the Appalachian Mountains in the United States of America are more rounded and not as elevated. The largest mountain range in the world is the Himalayas in Asia. Some of the highest mountains in the world are found in these ranges. A few tall mountains are isolated, like Kilimanjaro in Africa.

Mountains influence climate. They push hot air upward and can collect moisture (water) from the air. Have students locate the Indian Ocean and the Himalayas on a map. Explain that the creation of the monsoon wind over India is linked to the formation of the Himalayas and the Tibetan Plateau. This started about 20 million years ago, when the Indian tectonic plate pushed into the Asian tectonic plate. This started the formation of the Himalayas.

The American cordilleras cross the Yukon and British Columbia in Canada and continue as the Rocky Mountains and coastal ranges of the United States and Mexico in North America. Some of the names for this mountain range include the Rocky Mountains, the Sierra Nevada, the Cascades, the Sierra Madre Occidental and Sierra Madre Oriental. This cordillera runs through Central America and becomes the Andes in South America.

Other mountain ranges that students may try to find information on include the Caucasus, Carpathians, Caledonian Belt, Pyrenees, Urals and the Tasman Belt.

## Rivers

Rivers are parts of huge drainage systems that let extra water flow from the land into the sea or a lake. Rivers create many special environments around the world. Again, you can extend students and challenge them with the questions in this text. Or you can make up your own questions. Refer to the table in the Student Book and challenge the students with more questions, such as:

- What countries do the rivers flow through?
- Which cities do they serve?
- Can you find these rivers on a map?
- Can you find the source of each river?
- Can you find the mouth of each river, where it flows into the sea or a lake?

## Grasslands

A grassland is a place where the average yearly rainfall is enough to grow grass. Sometimes there is enough rain for a few trees to survive, and this is called a savannah. Rain may only come at certain times of the year. Droughts can also be common in grassland and savannah areas. A result is frequent fires. The fires may destroy young trees and maintain the grass.

In many parts of Papua New Guinea, people have made grasslands by burning and clearing. The same processes are happening in parts of Asia and around the Amazon and Orinoco river basins in South America. These are not natural grasslands, they are created by humans. They impact on the environment and natural resources.

Africa is famous for its grasslands. Discuss some of the animals found there with students and see what students can find out about them. (For example, they might choose from buffalo, cheetah, elephant, giraffe, gazelle, antelope, hippopotamus, leopard, lion, rhinoceros, wildebeest, gnu, warthog, zebra.) One exercise is to divide them into meat-eaters (carnivores) and grass-eaters (herbivores). Students can compare them with animals found in Papua New Guinea. Later students may come to see that some of these animals are icons of the grasslands.

There are other important grasslands in the world that students may wish to research. The steppes of Eurasia, the North American prairie and the pampas in Argentina, South America, are all temperate climate grasslands. They too support large herds of grass-eaters. Note that there were no horses in America until Europeans came about 400 years ago. Native Americans in both the north and southern grasslands quickly adapted to the horse. A 'gaucho' is a South American cowboy. In North America, similar roles are held by cowboys on the prairies and deserts.

## Deserts

The curriculum does not mention deserts, however they are important natural features. The key to deserts is that they are very dry. Some are cold and all deserts can have large temperature shifts between day and night. Often they are very cold at night and hot during the day.

## Forests

The three main types of forest found in the world are tropical, temperate and evergreen pine. All forests are under threat from human activities. Forests are vital areas of biodiversity and natural resources, and they contain large amounts of carbon. Destroying forests adds more carbon to the atmosphere.

## Biosphere

The biosphere is that part of the Earth that supports life. Students should understand that everything in the biosphere is interconnected. Changes in one part will impact on other parts.

## 8.1.2 How physical environments influence human settlement patterns in the world

## 8.1.3 The impact of resource use on the world's physical environments and human settlement patterns

## 8.1.4 International examples of sustainable practices to the natural environment and possible solutions to problems

### Main ideas

We cover three sections from 8.1.2 to 8.1.4 in the following material for teachers. In the Student Book, this covers people of the world, followed by resources around the world and then sustainable use of natural resources. These three sections are inter-related and have overlapping themes. The physical environment influences human settlement in many ways. The physical environments around the world impact on types of settlement and many types of human activities.

### Example of elaborating a learning outcome

**Strand:** Environment and Resources

**Sub-strand:** People and Environment

**Focus:** The effects of the physical environments on human settlement patterns in the nation and neighbouring regions

**Learning outcomes:**

**8.1.2:** Students are able to analyse how physical environments influence human settlement patterns in the world

**8.1.3:** Students are able to evaluate the impact of resource use on the world's physical environments and human settlement patterns

**8.1.4:** Students are able to identify international examples of sustainable practices to the natural environment and propose possible solutions to problems

- The teacher can have students make a timeline for world events as a possible elaboration. Students could use the blackboard, cardboard or paper to record measures and labels. Making a timeline is a way for students to understand how recently human settlement and human interaction with the Earth has occurred. The objective is for students to understand how short a time people have been on Earth and how great their impact has been.
- The teacher can give students the chance to develop their own scale for the timeline. The scale will show years in centimetres. Students can experiment with different scales. For example, what happens if students use one centimetre for 1 000 years? Or one centimetre for 1 000 000 years? If the scale is too big, the timeline will be metres long.

A possible elaboration for one week:

| Monday | Wednesday |
|---|---|
| *10 minutes of class time*<br>Students prepare a timeline of world events (see suggestions below). This work can be done by individuals, groups or the whole class, depending on resources. | *First half-hour of class*<br>Groups or individuals present their timelines and discuss how recently humans settled the world and how they use global resources. |

Suggested events for a timeline, based on what science has found so far, include:

| Events | Years ago |
|---|---:|
| The Earth starts to form as a planet that orbits the sun | 4 600 000 000 |
| The Earth's crust, oceans and atmosphere are forming | 4 400 000 000 |
| Meteorites stop hitting the Earth in large numbers | 3 900 000 000 |
| Bacteria is evident from fossil remains | 3 500 000 000 |
| Tiny organisms start producing oxygen using photosynthesis | 2 700 000 000 |
| Large continents start forming | 2 400 000 000 |
| Evidence of single-cell organisms existing | 1 450 000 000 |
| Evidence of sexual reproduction | 1 000 000 000 |
| Evidence of more complex life – worms, sponges, jellyfish | 680 000 000 |
| Animals with shells and skeletons appear in the oceans | 5 700 000 000 |
| Plants begin to appear on the land | 430 000 000 |
| Animals begin to appear on the land | 410 000 000 |
| Earliest dinosaurs appear | 290 000 000 |
| Early mammals (small animals like rats) start to appear | 250 000 000 |
| Flowering plants begin to appear on the land | 138 000 000 |
| Great extinction of dinosaurs | 63 000 000 |
| Early human ancestors appear in Africa | 7 000 000 |
| Age of earliest remains of modern humans (homo sapiens) found | 200 000 |

Students decide on the scale. Students must decide that one centimetre equals how many years? Then they make a timeline. If the scale is too big, the timeline will be metres long.

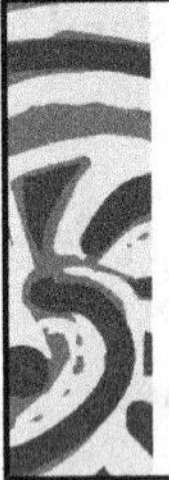

## Key words

Settling the world, world populationn, adapting to the physical environment, population distribution, population density, settlement patterns including archaeology, resources, sustainable practices

**Possible assessment tasks**

Examples of ideas are given in different categories. The same idea could be part of any category and teachers will develop other assessment tasks and further categories.

The following tasks can be done on paper or as an oral report by individuals or groups:

1 Report on what is happening to population growth around the world. What will happen as populations continue to grow for the next 40 years?

2 Collect articles on European cities and write a paper or give a talk about them.

3 Find information on aging populations. What countries or regions have aging populations? How does this compare with places where populations are youthful?

4 Explain the reasons why some places in the world are very densely populated and other regions are not.

5 Pollution from China blows all the way to the United States of America. Find and discuss other examples of how human activity impacts on the atmosphere right around the world.

6 Compare two very different places on Earth, such as Singapore and Mali. Make charts to show the differences and explain how people have adapted to these different environments.

7 Study any major natural resource of your choice, such as gold, oil, forests, copper, or soil.

8 Collect information and write a report about one type of renewable resource.

9 Collect information about the oil industry and see if you can find information about how oil companies are now investing in renewable energy technologies.

The following tasks can be done as role-plays by individuals or groups:

- Role-play the different ways that people in different parts of the world adapt to their environment.
- Role-play the advantages and problems of living in very densely populated areas. Then role-play the advantages and problems of living in very sparsely populated areas.

The following topics can be used for individual or team debates. Assess students on their ability to SEE (collect information), UNDERSTAND/ANALYSE (whichever side of the debate they are given) and ACT (present their side of the debate). Always debrief the class after the debates. Be sure they understand that there is no single right answer and that debates help improve knowledge whichever side you are on.

1 In the future, almost everyone will live in a city *versus* In the future people will start moving back to rural areas.

2 The Earth has more than enough resources for everyone if we use them carefully *versus* The Earth is a limited natural resource and people will have to sacrifice and make do with less to protect the Earth.

3 Population growth is good for the world *versus* Population growth is bad for the world.

The following tasks involve making posters or songs by individuals or groups:

1 Create a series of posters about the biggest cities of the world.

2 What do you think the ideal total population should be? Explain and illustrate your reasons on a poster.

3 Make a set of posters about the way early humans settled the world, starting in Africa around 200 000 years and moving to other continents around 70 000 years ago.

4 Make up a song about recycling and careful use of the world's resources.

5 Make up a set of songs about the way people live in cities in different parts of the world.

The following tasks can be done in a variety of ways by individuals or groups:

1 Collect information on food and use it to make posters, songs, role-plays or reports.

2 See how many uses you can find for each of these minerals: petroleum, lead, copper, zinc, bauxite (the ore for aluminium), titanium, coal, lithium, iron ore, magnesium, gold, silver. Present your information in a table, poster or another format of your choice.

## Teacher information

### Settling the world

Humans (homo sapiens) have only been on Earth for about 200 000 years. The earliest remains of modern humans have been found in Ethiopia. Modern human remains that date back to about 120 000 years ago have been found in South Africa. Modern human remains that date back over 90 000 years ago have been found in Israel, but this group seems to have died out. They seem to represent an unsuccessful migration from Africa.

Even earlier types of people can be traced back for several millions of years. Scientists have found human ancestors that date back to about 7 million years ago. (The Student Book provides some of the clues that have already been found in Africa about early humans.)

All our ancestors probably started to leave Africa around 70 000 years ago. Because world climates were colder, there was more land exposed from the sea. This would have made some travel easier. It is still uncertain just how the first people crossed larger bodies of water. Some scientists think that it was accidental. They think that the early migrants got caught accidentally by a flood or tsunami and floated across on debris like uprooted trees. Other scientists think that the first migrants had simple rafts. These scientists may be biased in thinking early humans could not make more sophisticated boats. This is a good area for discussion with your students.

There is evidence that people left Africa to come first to Asia and Australia. Europe was in the grip of an ice age and was settled by modern humans later (starting about 40 000 years ago). Then about 20 000 years ago, early Asians started moving into the Americas.

In 2007, genetic evidence published in the Proceedings of the Natural Academy of Sciences suggests that Asians played a larger role in colonising Europe than Africans. This is just one example of how science adds new information to our understanding of early human settlement. All we can be sure of is that more discoveries will continue in science for us to better understand our past.

You may wish to extend students and discuss some of the other early groups who settled the Earth before modern human beings. There were other groups in Asia, Europe and Africa. For nearly two million years, tool-making types of humans have left Africa. Stone tools and remains have been found in Europe and Asia that date from 1.5 to 1.8 million years old. All these types of humans have vanished. All that is left are fossils, bone and some stone artefacts.

Neanderthals were strongly built people who lived in Europe for about 200 000 years. Then they disappeared completely about 30 000 years ago. That means they were in Europe with modern humans for at least 10 000 years. Presently, scientists think that Neanderthals kept in small groups. Modern humans might have had links to larger groups to help in times of trouble. No one is sure what happened to the Neanderthals, but after 10 000 years of co-existing with modern humans, they had all disappeared.

Scientists have found the remains of a type of very small people on Flores Island in Indonesia. The adults only stood one metre tall. They lived on Flores from about 95 000 to 13 000 years ago. Modern human beings only arrived in Flores perhaps 50 000 years ago. The little people were there for about 45 000 years before modern human beings. It seems they lived together for over 30 000 years. Eventually, the little people vanished. Even today, people on Flores Island have stories about small hairy people who lived deep in the mountains on the island.

Another type of early human, homo erectus, lived on Java one and a half million years ago. Perhaps it was some type of homo erectus that travelled to Flores Island. Perhaps they became smaller people over time. The little people of Flores made stone points, probably for spears that have been found with their remains at a cave in Flores. They hunted a type of small elephant that lived on the island. The elephant weighed about 350 kilograms. They would have needed special skills to hunt such a big animal.

Students could find Flores and Java islands on a map. They could make a song or a story about what they think happened to the little people on Flores Island.

### Recent human settlement

After the first modern humans settled around the world, there is a long period of prehistory where different cultures and groups developed, but there is no time or space for this in the syllabus. In Chapter 2 of the Student Book, the story picks up again with the development of urban cultures. Students studied earlier settlements in the region and on New Guinea Island in Grade 7. The Grade 8 Student Book focuses on the last 400 years.

This was a period of expanding European and Asian colonialism. Millions of migrants came to North and South America from Europe first, and from Africa as slaves. Over time, Asians migrated in smaller numbers to the 'new world', as North and South America came to be called. Much smaller numbers came to the continent of Australia.

China expanded to the south and west to take over a number of territories. This ended only recently with the formal annexation of Tibet. Japan also colonised parts of China for a while, until defeated at the end of World War II in 1945.

Today streams of people continue to migrate around the world. Many are searching for better economic opportunities. Others are fleeing conflict and repression. They are refugees. Some are being forced to flee their land for their lives. This reflects a growing world population with conflicts over resources.

## World population

You can have students make graphs or tables to show the essential point of the growing world population. Here is the key information:

| Years ago | World population |
|---|---|
| 12000 | 10 000 000 or 1 000 000* |
| 1905 | 2 000 000 000 |
| 1959 | 3 000 000 000 |
| 1999 | 6 000 000 000 |
| 2050 | 9 000 000 000 |

* Note it really does not matter if you start with one or ten million, because the time is so long ago. Students may ask the maths teacher for help to construct this graph. The point is to show how fast modern humans are now populating the Earth. Populations should start to stabilise at nine or ten billion, according to scientific projections. The question is, what resources will all these new people need? This is a good discussion topic to elaborate on.

### Urbanisation

'Urban' refers to cities. More than half of the world's population now lives in cities. Students should be able to find information in the news about major cities in the world. It is important to understand that urban areas are now growing so large in some areas that cities are starting to merge into each other. This creates a 'megapolis'. The east coast of the United States of America is a good example. Students can locate Boston and Washington D.C on a map. In between, they will find cities such as Baltimore, New York and Newark making a megapolis well over 1 000 kilometres long. Tokyo and its port city, Yokahama are another example of a megapolis.

### Growing populations

Asia is the leader in population growth. This means that more resources are going to Asia. It links to the expanding economies of India and China. These countries have both tried to limit their populations. China has a one-child policy that is strongly enforced in many cities. It is not as strong in all rural areas. India tried a program of family planning that failed. At present rates, India will be the most populous country in the world by 2050. Again this has implications for resources and the environment. Will India be a threat to its neighbours, China and Pakistan? This is the type of question that students could explore by looking at news items about these countries.

### World population density

World population density is uneven. The key here is that very dense populations must be supported by basic resources: fresh water, productive land and clean air. Social organisation is also important. Have students study the map of world population density in the Student Book and analyse reasons for the areas where populations are most dense. They will need an atlas to find other information and give good explanations.

## Adapting to the physical environment

People have adapted to living in many places on Earth over the past 50 000 years, from sea level to mountain elevations just over 3 000 metres. People have adapted to very wet places, to very dry places, to very hot places and to very cold places. Students can find examples of different environments around the world, and how people have adapted to them. The Student Book gives some examples, here are two more:

- The Uygur people of the western deserts of China live in a very dry place. Their culture regards respect for water as very important. Respecting water helps to conserve it. Traditionally, when guests enter a home or dwelling, the host pours a little water on their hands. This lets them wash their hands and is a sign of respect by giving some very valuable water to the guest.
- Thai people live in a very densely populated environment because much of the country has highly productive soils. Enough food for everyone is important. Rice is the key staple in the Thai diet. In Thai culture, it is considered rude to waste even one grain of rice. This disrespects the hard work of the Thai farmers. It also makes people conscious of the need to use their food resources wisely.

There are many other examples of dress, architecture, transport and resource use adapted to particular environments around the world. One elaboration on this topic could be having students collect pictures to analyse what adaptations they show for particular locations and environments.

## Resources around the world

The Student Book can only look at a few of the resources around the world. You may use an atlas to study the location of world resources. Food and minerals are two examples of resources the class could study. Teachers could find many others.

### Food

The Student Book briefly covers food from the land and sea. There are many more examples and studies that can be made on food. This is an essential resource, and students should have no trouble understanding that.

## Case study: fisheries and aquaculture

Looking at fisheries and aquaculture helps us see how resources are changing. There are only so many fish in the oceans. They are a finite resource. There are two types of fisheries, freshwater and saltwater. Most of the world fish resources are in the sea. Around the world, more and more people are using these resources. Many fish resources are being over-used. In some places, the fish resources have been used up and the fisheries have been destroyed.

**Marine and inland fisheries capture 2002**

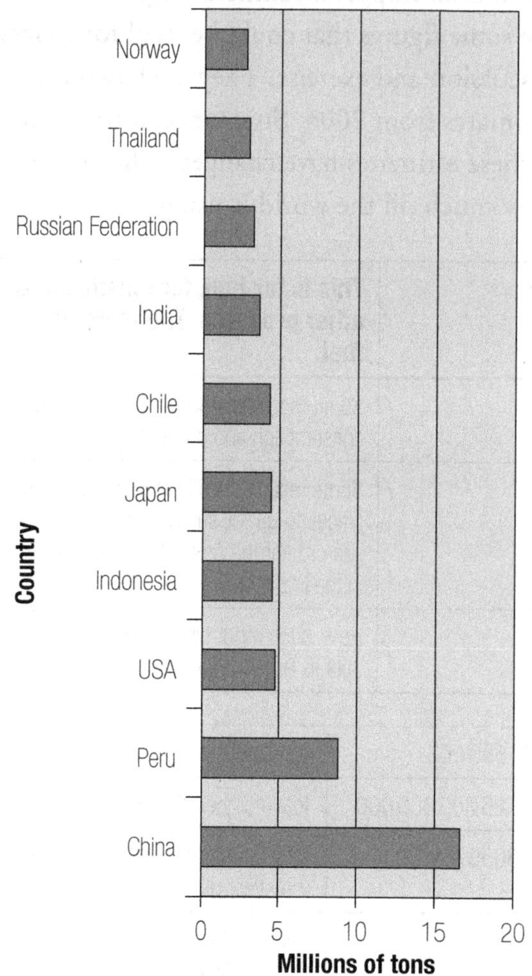


The ten countries in this graph capture about 60 per cent of the world's fisheries. In 2002, about 93 million tons of fish were captured (or taken by nets, hooks and traps) by the world fisheries. The biggest producers were China and Peru. About 90 per cent of this catch came from the oceans. The rest came from freshwater or brackish water. The question is, how long can world fisheries keep capturing 93 million tons of fish before this resource runs out?

One way to help the natural resource has been to stop killing unwanted fish. These fish are called 'trash fish'. Better nets and fishing practices now save one or two million tons of these fish each year, and keeps them in the food system for other sea creatures.

Another solution is aquaculture. It is a different type of resource use. Aquaculture is the term used for fish farming. It is used to grow prawns, shellfish and fish. It can be done in freshwater, saltwater or brackish water. The technology for aquaculture is growing too. People are learning how to grow different types of fish. Aquaculture is becoming more important and producing more food for the world.

Aquaculture can damage the environment if people are not careful. On the coast, it can destroy mangroves that are an important part of the coastal environment. Mangroves are the breeding places for many fish. They provide protection for baby fish to grow bigger. They protect against erosion. They protect against tsunamis. In other places, aquaculture helps protect the environment. Oyster farmers need very clean water or the oysters can be poisonous to eat. New technologies and better environmental protection will be needed for aquaculture to grow. Aquaculture produced about 40 million tons of fish, prawns and other shellfish (like oysters and clams) in 2002. Aquaculture also produced nearly 12 million tons of aquatic plants.

It is difficult to protect the ocean fisheries because nations must co-operate to make rules. Nations can control their own coastal waters if they have the money to protect them. But the high seas are free and anyone can fish on them.

For a fisheries study, or study of some other food, have students look in their local trade stores and food stores. What fish products can they find? What other products can they find from the sea or fresh water? Can they tell which ones come from aquaculture and which ones come from capture fisheries? Can they tell where the product comes from? Can they identify the country of origin and also the place where it was caught or raised?

Leaving the sea and moving to food production on land, we find that the Green Revolution has used science to greatly improve the production of many crops. There are costs in terms of fertiliser and pesticides. This is an area that some students may study further. Another area is the development of genetically modified crops. Some people are very worried about using them; other people see them as a saviour for starving people in the poorest places on Earth.

## Minerals

Minerals are unevenly spread around the world. Mineral wealth is often poorly distributed to the people around it. The most important mineral challenge is energy.

Oil is an important mineral resource. Here are some figures that could be used for a class discussion and exercise. They are based on estimates from 2004. Students can try to find if these estimates have changed. They show how much oil the world is using.

| **Estimated world oil production per day** | **82.590 million barrels** | **This is for fuel, for plastics and other products. The main use is fuel.** |
|---|---|---|
| Estimated world oil consumption per day | 82.6 million barrels | Some reserves are built, but generally consumption and production is very close. |
| Proven oil reserves | 1.326 billion barrels | Some reserves are in ever more difficult places to get to, such as deep under the sea or near the Arctic. Most reserves are in the Middle East. |
| Unproven oil reserves | Unknown | How much more oil will companies be able to find and how difficult will this be? |

Students can use the figures in the above table to see how many years of oil the world has left. They may need the maths teacher to help them. They can pursue questions like:

- How many years of oil are left if the rate stays the same? (See the table right.)
- If rates increase what happens?

| 82 590 000 | Use every day |
|---|---|
| 1 326 000 000 000 | Total number of barrels |
| 1 6055.2 | Total number of days (divide total by use every day) |
| 43.9 | Total number of years (divide total days by 365) |

People are still exploring for oil and gas. These figures are from 2004. The world is using more oil each year. Have the students look at the table of the ten biggest countries in the Student Book. Both India and China have rapidly growing economies that use oil and other energy resources. What difference might this make? There will be new discoveries, but they will probably be in very difficult environments. They will probably be small. World demand will keep increasing. We will use more each day not less at present rates.

## Sustainable use of natural resources

Growing populations are putting pressure on resources around the world. Technology is allowing people to make and have more and more resources. For example, Chinese factories have made enough business shirts for every person on Earth to have one. There is a cost to the land, water and air. The world is becoming richer but many essential resources are being damaged.

The challenge for the 21st century (2000 to 2099) is to sustain resource use. This will mean finding ways to keep the air and water clean and plentiful. It will mean using land and other resources wisely so that there will still be resources for all the world's people by the end of the century.

## Natural resources: renewable and non-renewable energy

Oil, gas and coal are non-renewable resources. The world is now looking at sustainable renewable energy sources. The Student Book provides a table on major renewable fuel sources for students to pursue.

# 8.1.5 The causes and effects of hazardous natural events in other parts of the world and how people respond to them

## Main ideas

There is a table in the Student Book showing some natural hazards that became disasters with large loss of life. In every case, people were not prepared for the event. Even so, the loss of life is minor compared with many other hazards. Review natural hazards in the Teacher Resource Books for Grades 6 and 7. Students can now begin to consider the consequences of both natural hazards, human hazards, and combinations of hazards.

Some hazards are part of the environment. Some are accidentally created by humans. Some are knowingly created as the price of economic development, like the tailings from mines. And some are purposely developed to destroy people and cities. The greatest hazard for young people in the developing world is traffic. The World Bank and other development organisations have come to realise that more lives are lost in transport accidents than in almost anything else. Diseases such as malaria, HIV/AIDS and tuberculosis are growing hazards all over the world. Conflict and warfare are also growing hazards. The production and distribution of small arms has created great hazards for some societies.

World hazards continue for humans. Populations and economies are growing around the world. People and all the features of the world are becoming more interconnected. Responses to hazards are becoming international.

## Example of elaborating a learning outcome

**Strand:** Environment and Resources

**Sub-strand:** People and Environment

**Focus:** Major world hazards

**Learning outcome 8.1.5:** Students are able to identify and describe the causes and effects of hazardous natural events in other parts of the world and how people respond to them.

A possible elaboration for one week:

| Monday | Friday |
|---|---|
| *Last 20 minutes of class*<br>The teacher presents articles that combine natural hazards with other issues studied. See examples. | *Half-hour*<br>Students report on what they have been able to find. |

Alternative schedule: adapt to your particular timetable but give students enough time to find current material about serious hazards in the world and to analyse how much is natural as how much is a human contribution.

Example 1: the following news extract shows how people have worked to create a natural hazard as a weapon of war. Fire and flooding have long been used as types of weapons.

## TSUNAMI BOMB NZ'S DEVASTATING WAR SECRET

25.09.1999 By Eugene Bingham

TOP-SECRET WARTIME EXPERIMENTS WERE conducted off the coast of Auckland to perfect a tidal wave bomb, declassified files reveal.

An Auckland University professor seconded to the Army set off a series of underwater explosions triggering mini-tidal waves [on the New Zealand Coast] in 1944 and 1945.

Professor Thomas Leech's work was considered so significant that United States defence chiefs said that if the project had been completed before the end of the war it could have played a role as effective as that of the atom bomb...

Papers stamped 'top secret' show the US and British military were eager for Seal to be developed in the post-war years too. They even considered sending Professor Leech to Bikini Atoll to view the US nuclear tests and see if they had any application to his work.

Ask students:

- What other natural hazards can be made and used against people?
- What types of beliefs and values do people need to create weapons that might drown whole cities with a weapon like a tsunami?
- What other weapons could be considered world hazards?
- What are the most dangerous hazards – human or natural? (Students might want to debate this.)

Example 2: the following news extract are about fire, which can occur naturally or as the result of human activity.

# CLIMATE CHANGE COULD FUEL CHINA'S FOREST FIRES

10.07.2007 By Ben Blanchard

CHINA COULD FACE WORSE forest fires and be more severely affected by wood-destroying pests this year because of global warming, a senior forestry official said on Wednesday.

'International weather experts predict that because of the double effect of global warming and El Nino, 2007 will be the warmest year ever and the forest fire prevention situation will be extremely serious,' Cao told a news conference.

China had a successful year fighting forest fires in 2006, with a drop of more than a third in damaged woodlands, though 41 people died, Cao said.

With average temperatures rising and rainfall dropping, the problem of protecting China's 175 million hectares (676,000 sq miles) of forests — an area the size of Libya — is a large one.

'The weather is getting hotter, the area of forested land is expanding and people are travelling around China more and more, so it's getting that much harder to prevent forest fires,' Cao said. 'We hope that improving early detection can help us.'

Yet that was being hindered by an attitude problem among some government officials at the grassroots, Cao said, particularly as most forest fires in China were caused by humans.

'The rise in disease is also related to global warming,' he added.

Ask students:

- What type of natural and human hazards is the official Cao talking about?
- How are they all inter-related?
- Find China on a map. Is it larger or smaller than New Guinea Island? Or Papua New Guinea?
- How similar are the hazards that Cao is talking about to ones in Papua New Guinea?
- What solutions does Papua New Guinea have for these types of problems?

**Key words**

global warming

## Possible assessment tasks

Examples of ideas are given in different categories. The same idea could be part of any category and teachers will develop other assessment tasks and further categories.

The following tasks can be done on paper or as an oral report by individuals or groups:

1 Explain how people in different parts of the world prepare for one of the following: earthquakes, tsunamis, volcanic eruptions, floods, storms and fires.

2 What is global warming and what are people doing about it around the world?

The following topics can be used for individual or team debates. Assess students on their ability to SEE (collect information), UNDERSTAND/ANALYSE (whichever side of the debate they are given) and ACT (present their side of the debate). Always debrief the class after the debates. Be sure they understand that there is no single right answer and that debates help improve knowledge whichever side you are on.

1 World leaders need to start action now to slow and then stop global warming *versus* World leaders can take more time to plan and have more important things to do than worry about global warming.

2 People cannot really prepare for hazards like tsunamis, earthquakes or cyclones *versus* People can prepare for natural hazards in many ways.

3 The greatest danger to the world is from natural disasters *versus* The greatest danger to the world is from disasters made by humans.

The following tasks can be done as posters or songs by individuals or groups:

1 Create a poster about one type of natural hazard and where it is found around the world. Include a map and newspaper articles.

2 Create a set of posters illustrating the greenhouse effect.

3 Create a poster that shows the countries that are most vulnerable to the impact of global warming. Provide information on what people can do to adapt to sea level rises.

4 Find examples in the news where people were not prepared for a natural hazard and write a song about it to sing to the class.

5 Write a song about human-made and natural disasters and what the results have been to sing to the class.

The following task can be done in a variety of ways by individuals or groups:

1 Collect information on natural hazards, human hazards and combinations of both. Analyse which is the most dangerous of the three different types of hazards.

# Teacher information

## Global warming

One of the biggest hazards that humans face is global warming, or climate change. It is caused both by nature and by human activity. Presently humans are causing more and faster global warming than nature.

Global warming is the heating of the Earth's atmosphere. The cause is an increase in greenhouse gases. There are three main gases – carbon dioxide, methane and water vapour. These gases trap heat from the sun.

This is the same as what happens to sunlight that passes through glass. The heat is trapped inside. Greenhouses are made of glass and rely on this principle to trap heat so that plants can be grown. Greenhouses are used to grow and protect plants in colder areas. They are not needed in most parts of Papua New Guinea, so students may not be familiar with the term.

Atmospheric scientists are the experts on greenhouse gases and their impact on the Earth's environment. Most agree that human activities have caused global warming for at least the last 100 years and that global warming is increasing in line with increasing production of greenhouse gases.

Many oil and coal companies do not like this news. They have said that the atmospheric scientists are giving false information in order to earn money studying greenhouse gases and global warming. There is no proof for this. It is clear that oil and coal companies may lose profits if charges increase for their products. These companies have sponsored scientists to counter the greenhouse claims.

Scientists, the public and politicians are now all tending to agree that global warming presents a major threat to many environments in the world. The size of the threat remains unclear. About 125 000 years ago, the global temperature was four degrees warmer on average and sea levels were four to five metres higher than today.

In coming years, there will be a greater international effort to reduce this threat and ensure the world does not get much warmer. Many of the problems in reducing carbon and methane gases will be related to lifestyles around the world. There are many discussion questions about global warming. They can also be discussed as part of Strands 2, 3 and 4:

- Will people want more air conditioning and big cars? (Both these items use up extra energy.) Or will they start to plan houses and buildings that are better adapted to the climate?
- Will people use more public transport and much smaller cars?
- Can governments be trusted to make and keep international agreements to reduce greenhouse gases?
- Is it fair to ask India and China to cut down on carbon dioxide emissions when their economies are just starting to be modernised?
- Should countries be paid not to chop down forests to help reduce carbon emissions?
- If governments do agree to pay for forest conservation, who should receive this money?
- What can students do to help reduce greenhouse gases?

# Organisation

## About this strand

This strand has one sub-strand, Social and Economic Organisation. In Grade 6, the focus was on the community. In Grade 7, it was on provincial, national and regional aspects of organisation. In Grade 8, the curriculum expands to cover the world's social and economic organisation. It looks at the past, present and future. Teachers will have to decide how much material students can absorb, and plan accordingly.

The sub-strand, Social and Economic Organisation, is divided into three sections. The ideas presented in the curriculum overlap. Teachers will be able to combine material that focuses on government and international trade. The three sections cover a wide range of ideas and information including:

- past and present governments and some of their achievements, ending with coverage of the United Nations
- past and present factors in international trade and forms of government
- ways to change trade and government that lead to social and economic development at the international level (the Student Book examines an example of one very positive world achievement in this area, the abolition of legal slavery).

Strand 2 covers extensive material. It examines different types of world governments in the past and present, and how governments have changed over many years. It selects and reviews some aspects of ancient history including early urban settlements when the world had a much smaller population. It gives an introduction into how people have now become more connected all over the world.

In previous grades, students have looked at some of the difficulties in world trade and this theme continues in Grade 8. It introduces some other aspects of international relations (other than trade) and looks at international co-operation. It examines how the world has started initiatives for peace and tried to break patterns of conflict and war. The Student Book breaks this material into a number of parts. This should allow students to grasp the main ideas more easily.

An 'Example of elaborating a learning outcome' is given for each section.

## 8.2.1 The form and origin of contemporary, traditional and constitutional government in other parts of the world

## 8.2.2 Conditions that have led to the present day international forms of trade and government

## 8.2.3 Changes to trade and government that would lead to social and economic development at international level

### Main ideas

There are many different types of governments in the world. Democracy is the most successful form of government today. In the past, there have been many other types of government. Some of these still exist today. There are strong and weak governments around the world. The United Nations has been created to encourage world peace and co-operation between all governments. This strand provides an overview to the United Nations and takes a slightly closer look at one of its affiliates, the World Health Organisation (WHO).

Governments have changed over time. Teachers will be able to point to many examples. Students will have seen examples of recent change too. We can learn from the past and students are given a brief history of settlement, government, economics and society around the world. This provides them with the beginning of a framework to understand the present and future. Students should come to understand that studying and understanding the past (or history) can help us to understand what is happening now. Students are given a brief historical base to put the present into context.

People are now more connected with each other than ever before. International trade, transport and communication connect everyone in the world. For example, students are now able to find news and other types of information that no one dreamed of having 100 years ago in Papua New Guinea.

World trade is rapidly growing. Students can find many examples of the advances that China is making in world trade. World trade is only one type of international relationship. There are many other forms of international co-operation and relations.

The world has made progress in improving social and economic organisation. Sometimes all news seems negative. But a balanced examination shows that more people now have more opportunities than ever before. The clearest example of world improvements is the abolition of legalised slavery. This chapter of the Student Book closes with a case study in how all the nations of the world have agreed to stop legalised slavery. This achievement brings thousands of years of human exploitation in its worst form to an end.

## Example of elaborating a learning outcome

**Strand:** Organisation

**Sub-strand:** Social and economic organisation

**Focus:** Governments past and present around the world

**Learning outcome 8.2.1: Students are able to identify and describe the form and origin of contemporary, traditional and constitutional government in other parts of the world**

**Learning outcome 8.2.2: Students are able to outline conditions that have led to the present day international forms of trade and government**

**Learning outcome 8.2.3: Students are able to suggest changes to trade and government that would lead to social and economic development at the international level**

A possible elaboration for one week:

| **Monday** | **Friday** |
|---|---|
| *Last half-hour*<br>Spend time with the class to have a discussion about the major items in the news that involve governments around the world. Evaluate a couple of news articles with the class.<br>Groups or individuals can collect more information on the news items or related or contrasting items for homework. Have the students use the See-Understand-Act model to see how the different parts of government are functioning in the items chosen. | *Up to one hour, depending on time available*<br>Have each group or individual report back to the class about:<br>– the information they have discovered<br>– how they have analysed it<br>– what it shows about government functions in another part of the world<br>– any bias they have noticed in the different information sources<br>– how the actions might influence people to vote in a democracy<br>– how it relates to other parts of the social science studies they have done. |

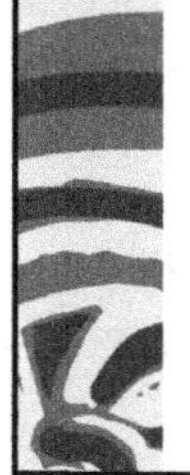

### Key words

governments around the world, structure or parts of governments, democracy, voting in democracies, dictatorship, fascism, monarchy, rotationism, communism, socialism, kleptocracy, constitutions, history, agriculture, complex social organisations, industry, science, technology, globalisation, the United Nations, international trade, products, protection, values, tourism, health, education

### Possible assessment tasks

Examples of ideas are given in different categories. The same idea could be part of any category and teachers will develop other assessment tasks and further categories.

The following tasks can be done on paper or as an oral report by individuals or groups:

1 Report on the changes to governments through history.

Organisation

2 Write a new speech for Martin Luther King Jr that covers different parts of the world where there is racism today.

3 Write a report or make a speech on the major areas of progress in the world compared with 100 years ago.

4 Write a report or give a talk to the class on what government is and how governments use their powers.

5 Review the many different types of government in world history then write or talk about the future of governments in the world and world government.

6 Write a report or give talk that compares the governments of China, India and the United States of America.

7 Write a report or give a talk on why countries want to protect their products from international competition but also want to sell their products around the world.

The following tasks can be done as role-plays by individuals or groups:

1 Do a set of role-plays on different types of governments in the world.

2 Do a role-play that shows how people around the world are much more connected compared with 200 years ago.

3 Do a role-play about different types of voting in democracies.

The following topics can be used for individual or team debates. Assess students on their ability to SEE (collect information), UNDERSTAND/ANALYSE (whichever side of the debate they are given) and ACT (present their side of the debate). Always debrief the class after the debates. Be sure they understand that there is no single right answer and that debates help improve knowledge whichever side you are on.

1 Debate with three teams: The executive part of government is the most important and powerful *versus* The legislature part of government is the most important and powerful *versus* The judiciary part of government is the most important and powerful.

2 Monarchies are a better form of government than dictatorships *versus* Dictatorships are a better form of government than monarchies.

3 Sometimes democracies have to take away human rights and have powers like dictatorships *versus* Democracies should always protect human rights first and never take them away from citizens.

4 A debate with three teams – each team takes one United Nations agency and debates that its agency is the most important. For example, United Nations Development Programme (UNDP) is more important than any other UN agency *versus* United Nations Educational, Scientific and Cultural Organisation (UNESCO) is more important than any other UN agency *versus* the World Health Organisation (WHO) is more important than any other UN agency *versus* United Nations Educational, Scientific and Cultural Organisation UNESCO is more important

than any other UN agency.

The following tasks involve making posters, models or songs by individuals or groups:

1 Create posters or maps to show where different types of government exist in the world today.
2 Create a set of posters that illustrate how different types of governments work today and in the past.
3 Make models of how early agriculture allowed the first cities to be built.
4 Make posters with maps to show the early civilisations on different continents and illustrate with pictures or drawings.
5 Write and sing some songs to the class about world trade and why it is so important for people, and some of the problems with world trade.
6 Write a song about the United Nations and what it is doing around the world.
7 Write a song about how the nations of the world stopped slavery and about other progress that the world has made.
8 Write a song to sing to the class that tells about monarchies, democracies, theocracies, socialism, dictatorship, fascism, and communism.
9 Write a song about the relationships between countries of the world over the last 100 years – how and when they have fought and how and when they have co-operated. The song can end with what the singer sees for the future.

The following tasks can be done in a variety of ways by individuals or groups:

1 Collect and present any materials you can find about early civilisations in a format of your choice.
2 Use posters, reports, models or songs to talk about any item (for example, a blouse, a tin of fish or a school desk) and explore how industry, science and technology have contributed to its production. How different would it be if you had to make it 500 years ago?

# Teacher information

## Governments around the world

Students have covered the basic concepts of government in Grades 6 and 7. They are now given an overview of the main types of government that rule in countries of the world today.

The number of nations in the world keeps changing. If you have access to the Internet, you can easily find information on the official United Nations website about all the member nations of the United Nations. In 2007, there were 192 members. This will change and you should check for new information if you can. Here is an example of all the member countries that have a name that starts with P, and the dates they joined the United Nations:

| Pakistan | 30 September 1947 |
|---|---|
| Palau | 15 December 1994 |
| Panama | 13 November 1945 |
| Papua New Guinea | 10 October 1975 |
| Paraguay | 24 October 1945 |
| Peru | 31 October 1945 |
| Philippines | 24 October 1945 |
| Poland | 24 October 1945 |
| Portugal | 14 December 1955 |

An important point for students to understand is that there are many ways to look at government. There are different definitions. There are many different ways to study government at different times or from different viewpoints. For example:

- Government can be defined as the legitimate use of power. This approach looks at how governments make laws and enforce them.
- Government is about organisation. It provides the means for services and protection within a country.
- Government is a type of social contract that people make. They agree to give the government power and privileges in return for protection and services.
- Government is a contest for power and resources. It is a struggle to get and keep power and access to a large share of resources.

## Structure or parts of governments

Students should understand that one way to study government is to look at the parts a government needs to rule. The teacher can lead a discussion on how these parts have changed over time. It is a fact that all around the world, governments have grown. They have more and more parts compared with earlier times. The three basic parts or branches of government are:

- Executive – the leaders (prime minister or president)
- Legislature – the law-makers (parliament, senate, house of representatives)
- Judiciary – the judges and courts (the justice system).

Modern democracies work to separate these three parts. This balances power among the three branches. It means that no single branch can make all the decisions. It provides a system where government decisions can be reviewed. This is important because governments do have power and power tends to corrupt. Having separate branches of government checks or reduces the power of any single branch. The text provides an introduction to a selection of different types of government. For the main types, have students search for examples of these governments' actions in the news media.

## Democracy

Democratic rule is the most common type of government today. The fundamental principle of democracy is that the people choose their leaders. There are many different ways to construct democracies based on this principle. In the United States of America, there are states where the people elect the president of the nation, the governor of the state, the legislators, the county judges and the county sheriff. In other democracies, not so many different roles are elected directly by the people.

The Student Book covers different types of voting systems. It also looks at how to balance different groups and interests with voting systems. There are many different voting systems in democracies. Voting can become very complex. It is open to being influenced by money or other resources. Groups can find many ways to influence votes for very narrow interests. Stopping corruption and improving good governance starts with an educated and interested group of voters, that is the electorate. Some students may wish to study different voting systems and compare different places. Some of the issues to consider are:

- How do you make every vote equal?
- How do you protect minority rights?
- How do you make people value their vote?
- How do you ensure people have a choice of good leaders to vote for?

## Dictatorship

Dictators are people who have absolute power in a country. This is the power of life and death. Human rights are very limited and generally abused in dictatorships. There are many examples of severe dictatorships over the last 100 years around the world. Joseph Stalin was the dictator of the Union of Soviet Socialist Republics (USSR) from the 1920s to the early 1950s. Adolph Hitler was the dictator of Nazi Germany from the 1930s to 1945. Both these dictators were responsible for the deaths of millions of people. Other dictators controlled parts of Europe, South America, Africa and Asia (including the Middle East) during the last century. Few remain today, although democracies in some of these places are very weak; for example, Pakistan has a history of shifting between democracy and military rule.

## Fascism

The fascist system of government started in Italy in the 1920s. The Italian fascist leader and dictator was Benito Mussolini. He was killed at the end of World War II by partisans who had turned against the fascist dictatorship. Germany was a powerful fascist nation in World War II until it lost in 1945. There were fascist parties in many other European countries just before World War II (even in Britain). The last fascists were in Spain and Portugal. They avoided fighting in World War II. Fascist government ended with the fall of the Salazar-Caetano regime in Portugal in 1974.

## Monarchy

A monarchy is based on hereditary rule. The leader is born to the position. It is ascribed, not earned. The idea of hereditary rule was never very strong in Melanesia, where the right to rule was generally earned in each generation. But hereditary rule was established for long periods in many other parts of the world. Kings and queens ruled China and much of Asia for thousands of years. The Aztec, Maya and Inca civilizations of the Americas relied on hereditary rule. In fact the term 'Inca' was the title given to the ruler and it is similar in meaning to 'king'.

Europe has a long history of hereditary rule with kings, queens, tsars, kaisers and other titles given to leaders who were born to the position. The great weakness of the hereditary systems is that they limit the pool for leaders. Only those with royal or special blood can marry into the system. The result can be sub-standard leadership. Students can go all the way back to the Bible to see how kingdoms collapsed over and over again.

There are very few hereditary rulers left today in the world. There are a number of royal families but their right to rule is extremely limited or symbolic. In many cases, they are a cultural tradition that people like to keep and follow. Students could look at royalty as an elaboration on cultural expression and government (Strands 2 and 3).

The kings of Tonga and Lesotho (pronounced 'Lesutu') and the Council of Chiefs in Fiji are examples of hereditary rulers that still have some power. Jordan and Saudi Arabia in the Middle East still have powerful royal families in a region where democracy is not strong in many governments. Students can find articles about these places to see what is happening there.

### Rotationism

Rotationism is a good example of what can happen to weak democracies. The problem occurs when corruption and individual interests replace the national interest. This happened in Portugal for about 40 years starting in 1880. One government would stay in power until it was so weak that it rotated with another one. And the next one would change or rotate again. It was finally replaced by a fascist dictatorship that ruled for 50 years.

### Communism

Communism is based on state ownership. The government owns almost everything. The most severe example today is in North Korea. Communism is a type of dictatorship. Like many dictatorships, it seeks to control what people believe. This included religion in the past and is still the case to varying degrees in different communist countries today.

### Socialism

Socialism is an economic theory that gives control and ownership of the means of production to the community. It becomes a type of government when this control is passed to government. This is a type of government that controls much of the land and other means of production. Socialism is not based on a dictatorship, like communism. It can be a type of democracy. There have also been communities in Europe, the United States of America and Australia that tried to practise socialist principles within their country. Usually they have lasted only a generation (around 20 years) and then been absorbed into the larger society. New groups spring up and some are functioning today. Sometimes they may be based on a religious cult or on a non-religious philosophy of community sharing.

All modern democracies have some forms of socialism. They use taxes to redistribute wealth. The wealthy democracies provide a safety net for people who have no money or other resources. This ensures that they do not die of hunger and receive basic medical care. Less wealthy countries still rely on community, family, clans or religious organisations or other non-government means to provide a safety net. All these are a form of socialist practice in redistributing wealth.

### Kleptocracy

Kleptocracy is a recent term to describe some weak and corrupt governments that take more from citizens than they give. This can be a military dictatorship or a weak democracy. 'Klepto' is a Greek word that means 'to steal' and a 'kleptomaniac' is a person who tries to steal everything. A kleptocracy steals from the people.

### Theocracy

'Theo' is the Greek word and 'deo' is the Latin word for 'god'. A theocracy is a nation ruled by religious leaders who interpret the word and rules of their god. The supreme leader in this system of government is their god. Tibet was a type of theocracy until it was taken over by China in 1954. In ancient times, the leader of the country was often thought to be a god. That is also a type of theocracy. The Pharaohs of Egypt were also considered to be gods. Today, Iran is a good example of a theocracy. The religious leader, the Supreme Ayatollah, interprets the word of the Islamic god. The courts and laws are based on Islamic law. There are groups of people all around the world who would like governments to reflect their religious values; Christians, Hindus and Jews all have groups that promote theocratic ideas.

### Constitutions

A constitution provides the fundamental or organic rules for a government. Constitutions are written legal documents that form the basis for governments to rule. Weak governments may not follow their constitutions. Corrupt leaders may not follow their constitutions.

## A short history of the world

The curriculum covers a large amount of material in looking at the history of government and human settlement. Teachers can give students an overview. It will be hard to balance time and place. China, India and the Middle East are all places with claims to some of the earliest civilisations and complex social and economic organisation.

Over the last 2000 years there have been major civilisations and developments on every continent other than Antarctica. Much of the history has been lost or is seen only through the eyes of the winners. The history of places built of wood or bamboo or other perishable material is often lost. Remnants in stone help preserve some records. Even then, the materials can be destroyed – this is what happened to much of Egypt where temples were recycled for building materials in the 1800s and mummies were pounded up as a medicine or even fertiliser.

Another problem with the history of government is who writes the history? Bias and prejudice is found in many histories. The winners often write the history of wars. Ask students what type of bias or prejudice they think they would find in these histories.

### The first governments

Governments started in Africa with the first people. There are no records. This is a good area for students to discuss. Ask:

- Did early humans have leaders and forms of government?
- Was it only with modern humans from 200 000 years ago that government started?
- What would the early governments make decisions about?
- How would the early governments rule?
- What do you think the role of religion was in early governments?

The Student Book covers the basic movement of people around the world. This table can be used for discussion and questions on the very first human settlements and types of government.

| Time | Event |
|---|---|
| About 4 to 5 million years ago | First hominids (modern humans' ancestors) found in Africa |
| About 2 million years ago | The first homo (human) species found in Africa: homo habilis (the human toolmaker or handyman) |
| A little less than 2 million years ago | The first human species where some members migrate from Africa to Asia (and later to Europe): homo erectus has the intelligence to build shelters, use fires and makes more sophisticated tools, especially for hunting |
| Around 1.6 million years ago | Evidence of the homo erectus using fire in Africa |
| Around 1 million years ago | Evidence of homo erectus living in China: the Yuanmou man |
| About 300 000 years ago | Ancient or archaic homo sapiens appear |
| Around 200 000 thousand years ago | Emergence of modern homo sapiens in Africa |
| Around 70 000 years ago | Modern homo sapiens leave Africa and successfully start to colonise the world until all other types of humans like homo erectus, archaic homo sapiens and Neanderthals disappear forever. Genetic evidence now points to some mixture of the early African migrants with earlier Asian peoples. |

## Agriculture and government

Agriculture provides a basis for more complex forms of government. This leads to more complex forms of social and economic organisation. Agriculture provides a secure food supply when people adapt it correctly to the environment. Learning how to do this can take time. Failure to maintain secure food supplies is one way that governments and settlements can fail. The Student Book moves across world history with a few examples of some of the major civilisations of the early world:

- The Fertile Crescent made by the Tigris and Euphrates rivers: this is where the Mesopotamian civilisations started. It is often thought to be the place described as the Garden of Eden in the Bible. Cities began here and it may also be the place where writing first began.
- Ancient Egypt: the civilisation of Egypt is based on the Nile River. Usually the Nile would flood every year. People counted on this to replenish the soil. Sometimes the flood was much greater than expected and this could cause damage. Sometimes it was much less than expected and this could cause food shortages. Egyptians kept massive written records. Egypt is the other place where writing may have first started in the world. They started with a system called 'hieroglyphics', and modified it over time to include other types of writing like our cursive and printed writing today. The major concern of Egyptians was the afterlife and government spent much of its money on preparing for the afterlife of the Pharaoh (king) and other high officials.
- Ancient Greece and Rome: two important early civilisations in Europe. The Greeks had a number of countries or city-states. They provided many of the ideas and sciences that spread around Europe and other parts of the world. One of the Greek city-states, Athens, developed the first democracy. The electorate (the voters) in Athens was a minority of the population, as the majority of adults were slaves without a

vote. This was the basis of the early Greek economy. The Roman Empire conquered the Greeks and used Greek knowledge and culture to add to their own culture. The Roman Empire eventually conquered much of Europe and parts of Asia. The western part of the Roman Empire collapsed around 410 as German tribes attacked the city of Rome. The eastern Roman Empire, called the Byzantine Empire, was centred in Constantinople in what is now Turkey. Islamic forces finally conquered it in 1054. (Islam then had its own great empire that rose and fell.)

- China: China was ruled by various dynasties for thousands of years. A key part of Chinese government has been large bureaucracies. They were used for extensive record-keeping to ensure the smooth functioning of government. As with Egypt, China saw periods of unrest and internal fighting that led to the change of dynasties.
- The Americas: early civilisations developed in the Americas over several thousand years. In North America, many of the civilisations with names like Olmecs, Toltecs and the Aztecs were found in Mexico. Another group was the Mayans. The Mayan civilisation covered parts of Central America and Southern Mexico including the Yucatan peninsula, Belize and Guatemala. The Mayans also had writing and a very accurate calendar. In South America, the Spanish found the Inca civilisation in the highlands of the Andes. The Inca Empire extended over several thousand kilometres. There were many other South American civilisations, including the Chibchas in what is now Colombia, and other peoples along parts of the Pacific coast in what is now Peru. There may also have been extensive settlement and civilisation in the Amazon basin. Disease wiped these people out completely. This also happened to many indigenous groups in North America and other parts of South America.

## The past 500 years

The Student Book quickly reviews the past 500 years. This is the period of European expansion. The Islamic Empire was in decline during this time, having had a very important period before. It is important that students understand that the people of Islam often lived under very tolerant rulers that allowed other religions like Christianity and Judaism to exist freely.

Like the Roman and Islamic empires before them, different European countries established their empires based on colonies. The Spanish and Portuguese started the process. The British, Russians and French followed with other countries like Sweden and the Netherlands all competing for colonies and territory. In Asia, China also expanded its territory during this period. In the late 1800s and early 1900s there was a final frantic land grab. Almost all of Africa was claimed by European nations, as were the Pacific islands and much of Asia. Japan took Pacific islands from Germany at the end of World War I, and invaded parts of China in the 1930s.

With the end of World War II, a long period of de-colonisation and the break-up of countries followed. Every decade now, we see new countries appear. Teachers can challenge students to find what the latest independent nations are. These will continue to change over time. One way to look for change is to find older maps; for example, a ten-year-old map will be different to a map of the nations of the world today.

## Industry, science and technology

Industry, science and technology have developed the means to bring everyone on Earth closer over the last 500 years. This started with the Industrial Revolution and the development of mechanical power. Today, 'globalisation' is a term that is often used to describe the impact of industry, science and technology on the world.

## Globalisation

Globalisation connects people all over the world with products and ideas. It allows everyone to trade and share products. There are benefits to globalisation, for example:

- opportunities for more people from more countries to trade internationally
- the exchange of important goods like medicines, computer systems, mobile telephone systems and learning materials
- the ideals of universal human rights to protect minorities or the oppressed
- an increase in wealth for people all around the world.

There are also critics of globalisation. Students can study both sides of the argument.

## The United Nations

The United Nations (UN) started at the end of World War II. Teachers should refer to Strand 4 for more information. The UN is covered in the curriculum in both Strand 2 and Strand 4, where it is proposed as one area for an integrating project if a student is interested in this.

## International trade and products

Another idea to help world peace and development is fair trade. International trade is important to every country in the world. Teachers may wish to review the issues covered in Grades 6 and 7. The idea of trade promoting peace has a Papua New Guinea context. In pre-colonial times (*taim bilong tumbuna*), groups would often trade or fight with each other. Trade was a time of peace. This same idea is promoted for international trade today. Additionally, the theory of international trade is that each country can produce what it is best at and buy the best from everyone else.

## Protection

All countries protect some aspects of trade. One reason is food security. This means that a nation needs to be able to produce enough food to feed its people in time of conflict or emergency. Another aspect is democracy. If a voter block is worried about their industry or market, they can vote out a free-trade government.

## Values

There are many biases and prejudices in trade. Each group generally thinks of its own interests first. Many people argue for protection and then complain when their own products are kept out of an international market. The United States of America, the European Union, China and India all protect parts of their trade and work tirelessly to promote their own products to the world. Students will be able to find many examples in the press and among the public on attitudes about trade. They can provide material for a class discussion: free trade or protection?

The Student Book shows that trade issues have been around since at least 1776. There is a selection by the first political economist, Adam Smith, from his famous book, *The*

*Wealth of Nations*. Students should understand that the American colonies had just begun their revolt against the British Empire in 1776. A major reason for the revolt was trade. The American colonies were being forced to trade on poor terms with Britain and they were being heavily taxed with no democratic representation in the British Parliament. The Adam Smith selection in the Student Book could be the start of an elaboration or integrated student project that could go in many different directions depending on the student's interest. There will be new material continually available in newspapers and the press to discuss these types of issues. Refer to the news item in the Student Book on page 138. Here are some examples of discussion questions that could follow a news item like this:

- What values are expressed or implied in this article?
- What do you think the Thai values about trade would be in this case?
- What are Minister Patteson's values?
- What would Solomon Island village values be?
- What do you think is more important: village people being able to buy cheaper canned tuna from Thailand or jobs for one village in the Soltai Fishing Company?
- How could you make a balanced study of these problems?
- What values are being shown in having a province own a business?
- Should governments own businesses?
- Why does the tuna need to be canned?

## International products

The Student Book looks at four products that are found in Papua New Guinea and their part in world trade today: passion fruit, mangos, chillies and coffee. There are many other products that a student could choose to research. Sugar, rubber, cacao, copra, tropical timber, oil, gold, copper, fish and cardamom are just a few examples with links to Papua New Guinea.

Map work can be part of following products around the globe. Trade can also be looked at in reverse by having students finding objects in trade stores or at home then try to trace them back to their places of origin. This will be very hard, particularly when trying to determine where all the ingredients in a tin come from, as well as the materials to make the tin and the label. It will give students some idea of just how complex world trade really is (and why it is often much easier and more economic to export raw materials).

The Student Book briefly examines why some countries manufacture goods and some countries export raw materials. But there are many reasons why countries export raw products. Here are some of them:

- The markets for processed products may be far away. Transport costs become too high, especially if you have to bring in materials to add to your raw product. (For example, where would you get the glass bottles for chilli sauce? It would be expensive to make them or import them.)
- There may be little expertise for this type of processing. For example, Singapore is a major processor or raw materials. Its oil refineries produce fuel products for much of Australia, New Zealand and Oceania. It has

brought in many people with special skills. It invests a lot of money in its education system from primary schools to universities.

- There may be labour shortages or expensive labour. China is one of the world's great manufacturers today. Chinese workers can produce many things to sell around the world. Chinese wages are very low. The working hours are long. This lowers the price of the processed goods. And the Chinese have more workers than any other country. It is hard to compete against them.
- Money is needed to process goods and sell them. In many places there is not enough money. Sometimes there is not enough protection for the people who have money. They could invest money in processing, but they think it is safer for them to invest somewhere else. Sometimes they will invest in other countries that they think are safer.
- Many countries try to protect their workers. They will not let processed goods into the country without adding customs costs. That can make a product too expensive to sell. Europe and the United States of America do this with agricultural products too. They are protecting their own farmers and stopping free trade.
- All countries have some standards that imported products should meet. Sometimes the safety standard can be very high. This can keep products out of the market or make them more expensive.

## Tourism, health and education

World trade is growing where people travel to a country for the service or product (rather than importing it to their country of origin). International tourism, health and education are all rapidly growing businesses. Papua New Guineans have travelled to Australia, New Zealand, the United States of America and countries in Europe for education. Universities in all these countries are competing for international students. The French have even agreed to teach in English in order to attract more international students to academies in Paris.

A more recent and expanding international business is in health services for middle class citizens. The very rich have always been able to seek the best health services. The newer business is for less rich people who are travelling for dental and medical services. China, Thailand and India are three important new countries providing these types of services. There are some dangers and negative consequences. A high-level Canadian team has accused some Chinese hospitals of organ harvesting. This means killing political dissidents to take their organs for sale as transplant parts. Very poor people in India have been induced (or sometimes forced) to give up a kidney for which they receive very little money. All the profits go to the hospital where the international health business is being conducted. A few doctors in Brazil have been accused of murdering people to take their organs for transplanting businesses.

Because of the way the statistics are recorded, international tourism is one of the largest international industries. All business travel is counted as a type of tourism, even though most people think of tourism as recreational. In the last section of the Student Book, covering Strand 4, more information is given on tourism as an example of some of the issues an integrated study could cover. Teachers can refer to that material if they wish to elaborate or cover more on tourism in Strand 2.

### Changes in government and trade

War, colonialism, bad trade deals and weak governments may give students a negative outlook. This needs to be balanced. The world today is a less cruel place than it was 100 years ago or 500 years ago when people thought that torturing animals for amusement was a good way to live. The world has made progress in many areas. The Student Book for Strand 2 closes with a case study on the slave trade, which shows how international relations, world trade and human rights have changed. The biggest change to governments and trade in the last 200 years is the abolition (or stopping) of legal slavery. There are still some problems with illegal slaves, but all legal slavery has been wiped out. Illegal slavery is often referred to as 'people trafficking'. Much of it involves taking young women and sometimes children from very poor places like Nepal, the Philippines, Laos, or northern Thailand. Usually they are promised a good job and then forced to do sex work. Another type of slavery is child labour and debt bondage. Very poor people sell their children to be servants or labourers. This is still a problem in some parts of Asia and Africa. Teachers can decide to what extent they may wish to explore these modern problems. The essential message for students is that all slavery is now illegal. What remains is a crime – like murder, robbery or fraud.

The Student Book closes with an examination of equal rights for all people and a selection of phrases from Martin Luther King Jr's speech known as 'I Have A Dream'. Martin Luther King Jr led peaceful demonstrations for equal rights for black Americans. Racists assassinated him and the struggle for equal rights for minorities continues in many countries. Here are a few additional phrases from Martin Luther King Jr's speech that teachers may use to more fully discuss his contribution and ideas:

- '...One hundred years later, the Negro lives on a lonely island of poverty in the midst of a vast ocean of material prosperity. One hundred years later, the Negro is still languishing in the corners of American society and finds himself an exile in his own land ... '
- 'I have a dream that one day on the red hills of Georgia the sons of former slaves and the sons of former slave owners will be able to sit down together at the table of brotherhood ... '
- 'I have a dream that one day even the state of Mississippi ... will be transformed into an oasis of freedom and justice ... '

# Culture

## About this strand

This strand has one sub-strand: Cultural Expression. This strand has three parts that can easily be combined to challenge students to identify and describe the basic features of some other cultures far from Papua New Guinea; discuss similarities and differences in cultures from around the world; and identify cultural changes around the world. The teacher can combine all three outcomes in the lessons that follow on aspects of culture from around the world. We do not separate them out. In fact, the first two learning outcomes are inseparable.

The Student Book provides two major approaches to studying cultures around the world and the concept of international or global culture. There is considerable text, which covers a number of ideas about culture around the world. Teachers and students can expand on any and all of these themes as well as search out many more. There are two sets of colour pictures, and each set looks at culture in a different way. However, you can use both sets for comparisons and to extend ideas and themes about culture around the world.

The first set of pictures looks at cultures through universal themes. The pictures can be sorted or combined differently to look at other themes or build on the existing themes. For example, the concept of gender as part of culture can be studied in every picture. Similarly the concepts of education and communication as a part of culture will have some aspect in every picture.

The second set of pictures looks at places of cultural significance. They are iconic places or icons of culture. They define some of the essence of special cultural differences. They show how all cultures from around the world have been able to create unique cultural expressions. But they can still be combined in different discussions with the first set of pictures. One exercise would be to challenge the students to find links and explain them between the two sets of pictures.

# 8.3.1 Comparing elements of other national cultures with our own

# 8.3.2 Identifying key elements that shape international culture

# 8.3.3 Participating in international culture

## Main ideas

There are cultural differences all around the world. At the same time, there is a growing international or global culture that people are sharing around the world. You can see this in responses to natural hazards. The most distant and isolated peoples on Earth can still get some assistance in the event of a major natural hazard. The Asian Tsunami flooded remote islands in the Indian Ocean where people have very little cultural contact with anyone else. Still they were provided with some assistance. Similarly, most people around the world now have some items from overseas. It may only be a pair of shorts, a cutting blade or a blouse but it is part of international or global culture. And many people share many things from around the world: songs, ideas, movies, stories and numerous physical items.

### Example of elaborating a learning outcome

**Strand:** Culture

**Sub-strand:** Cultural Expression

**Focus:** Cultural expression around the world

**Learning outcomes:**

**8.3.1: Students are able to compare elements of other national cultures with our own**

**8.3.2: Students are able to identify key elements that shape international culture**

**8.3.3: Students are able to participate in national culture**

Several possible elaborations are given in the example below. You may create other elaborations that connect material in the first two chapters to this chapter. Students can be challenged with elaborations that explore connecting questions such as:

- How are different cultural expressions linked to the environment and the way people treat the environment?
- How do sacred places of cultural expressions impact the environment around the world?
- What type of cultural expressions in other parts of the world assist to protect the environment?
- How is cultural expression linked to government and trade?

| Monday | Friday |
|---|---|
| *20 to 30 minutes*<br><br>Divide the class into three groups. Have each group choose pictures from three of the themes covered on pages 85 to 92. Have them show links between cultural items in the pictures. Assign each group one major area of the world:<br><br>The Americas, Europe or Asia. Set students the homework task of collecting more pictures from their assigned area to expand on the ones in the book. Allow all the groups to find pictures on the themes from Africa and Australia/Pacific Islands.<br><br>Alternatively, explain to students that all cultures have some things that are the same. For example there is shelter in every culture although there are many different types. People can recognise shelter, even when it is very different from their own. For example, an ancient Greek historian called Xenophon travelled to a place where the people lived underground 2 400 years ago. He had never thought this possible or had seen such places before. But he instantly recognised this as a type of shelter made by a different culture. Similarly today, in the Bird's Head region of New Guinea (the far west of the Indonesian provinces), people live in tree houses. Tents, igloos, wooden houses and stone houses are all types of shelters used by different cultures around the world.<br><br>Have the students choose a physical item (a part of physical culture) and try to find examples of it on every continent. Students can then discuss and explain what cultural differences or changes there are between places. The item could be as simple as a hairbrush, or vehicles, tables, basic food stuffs, clothing or much more complex physical expressions like cities or farms. Ask:<br><br>What are the reasons for change? (Environment, resources, values and other reasons can all be explored by students to explain some of the differences they find.) | *One-half to one hour*<br><br>Have each group present the pictures they have collected. Have them explain how the pictures are related and what aspects of culture they are showing. Ask:<br><br>What is similar and what is the same in these features of cultures?<br><br>What changes can be seen in the cultures?<br><br>What do the new pictures and the existing pictures tell us about some part of the text in Chapter 1 or 2 (or in both)?<br><br>What connections will you expect to see in the future?<br><br>How different are the expressions of the theme in Africa and Australia/Pacific Islands?<br><br>Alternatively, ask the same questions as above, but open them up to all the continents. The material does not have to refer to anything in the Student Book. |

## Key words

culture, world culture, cultural change, globalisation, continents, African cultures, European cultures, Latin cultures, North American cultures, South American cultures, Asian cultures. Australian cultures, cultural icons, melting pot, multiculturalism, religion, language, culture wars, stereotypes, the Internet, cultural items, myths, history, the Ancient Seven Wonders of the World, destroying world culture, protecting world cultural heritage

## Possible assessment tasks

Examples of ideas are given in different categories. The same idea could be part of any category and teachers will develop other assessment tasks and further categories. Teachers can work with students to decide on other possible assessment categories to include cultural performance.

The following tasks can be done on paper or as an oral report by individuals or groups:

1 Choose a culture in a country or region far from Papua New Guinea and compare it with cultures that you know about in Papua New Guinea.

2 Report on countries that are trying to preserve their cultures and compare this with places where the countries are trying to change the culture.

3 Make a list of international or global culture that you can find in Papua New Guinea. Choose five items from your list and report on where these came from originally.

4 Collect examples of how different cultures adapt to their environments. The report can have pictures or drawings.

5 Report or give a talk on cultures in one continent.

6 Try to find out the history of any one of the following items and then see how it has changed cultures around the world: radios, electricity, telephones, trucks, television, paved roads.

7 Report on the global influence of one religion or language. How has it added to or changed cultures around the world?

8 Report on the times and places when important parts of culture have been destroyed and suggest solutions to prevent the loss of the most valuable cultural items.

The following tasks can be done as role-plays by individuals or groups:

9 Do role-plays to give examples of how culture spreads and changes in different parts of the world.

10 Do a role-play about the development of writing and books that shows how the printing press changed cultures around the world.

11 Do a role-play of carnival (carnivale) from some part of Latin America (this can includes Mardi Gras in New Orleans as it has a Latin heritage) and then discuss in class what is similar and what is different to celebrations in Papua New Guinea.

12 See what other information you can find about Admiral Zheng , the famous Chinese explorer. Do a role-play about his life and the reasons that China stopped explorations to preserve the Emperor's culture and way of life.

13 Do a role-play of any Greek myth or story.

14 Do a role-play of a press conference that gives news about changes to culture around the world.

The following topics can be used for individual or team debates. Assess students on their ability to SEE (collect information), UNDERSTAND/ANALYSE (whichever side of the debate they are given) and ACT (present their side of the debate). Always debrief the class after the debates. Be sure they understand that there is no single right answer and that debates help improve knowledge whichever side you are on.

15 The printing press was the single most important innovation to change culture around the world *versus* The internet is the most single important innovation to change culture around the world.

16 Human culture started with language, that is what defines culture *versus* Human culture started with tools and language only came later.

17 We share most of our attitudes and beliefs with many other people in the world *versus* Very few of our attitudes and beliefs in Papua New Guinea are the same as in other parts of the world.

18 Secular (not religious) icons like Mickey Mouse and the American flag are the most recognisable cultural icons around the world *versus* Religious icons like the Virgin Mary are the most recognisable icons around the world.

19 The 'melting pot' approach, where everybody becomes part of a single national culture, is the best approach for countries to take with new migrants *versus* The multicultural approach, where everybody continues to practice their own culture as part of the national culture, is the best approach for countries to take with new migrants.

20 It is important to preserve as much of the different world cultures as we can *versus* A lot of world culture is not very good and we should not try to save it, rather we should encourage changes for new and better cultures.

The following tasks involve making posters, models, songs or pictures by individuals or groups:

1 Make posters or models of what you think the first cultures were like on Earth in Africa and then Asia, Australia, Europe, North and South America.

2 Make a series of posters or models to show some of the most important features of any of these themes in cultures from around the world: the arts (painting, music, literature), houses or shelters, rural settlements, ceremonies and rituals, language, sports, work and employment.

3 Do a series of posters that show different aspects of cultures on each continent.

4 Do a series of posters to show how people can prevent cultural stereotypes.

5 Collect articles about globalisation and make a song about it to sing to the class.

6 Look at the different types of singing in different cultures and then try to use some of the different styles to make songs about Papua New Guinea.

7 Find information about important world cultural places that need protection and write a song about them to sing to the class.

8 Teachers can divide the class into groups to collect pictures on different cultural themes for displays.

The following tasks can be done in a variety of ways by individuals or groups:

1 Collect pictures of cultural icons from around the world and explain how they represent the cultures.

2 Make a piñata and use it to recreate a Mexican birthday party.

3 Build a model, make a report or make posters about any one of the Ancient Seven Wonders of the World.

4 Build a model, make a report or make posters about any one of the Modern Seven Wonders of the World.

# Teacher information

## Culture

Culture is a very broad concept in social science. It includes the common ways that people think and act in a society. It includes all the physical objects that the society uses or makes. This is often called the physical culture. Culture spreads and changes. Cultures grow, cultures can decline and disappear, cultures can mix. We really do not know where some parts of our culture came from. The original people and their ideas have vanished, but we are still carrying some traces of them in our cultures today.

### World cultures

A teacher could spend a lifetime describing and discussing different cultures with students. Teachers will have to see what resources are available. In some places you may be able to get a guest speaker from overseas to speak about their culture. An Indian worker, an American volunteer, or an Israeli tourist could all be potential speakers to give the class a living idea about some of the differences in world culture. Be sure to question any guest speakers about what is similar in their culture to the cultures of Papua New Guinea. Guest speakers could use the first set of eight colour pictures to make comparisons with their culture. And students could interview the guest (or guests) to with questions like:

- In your country, how many different cultures are there?
- What type of group beliefs and values are found in your national culture (or cultures)?
- Can you explain attitudes, ways of doing things, roles, relationships and responsibilities that are typical in your culture?
- What do you have that is the same and different from us in the physical objects of your culture?
- What have you found most different about the cultures in Papua New Guinea?

Use these types of questions to discuss issues found in other sources about culture, even if you do not have a guest speaker. Use sources such as books, magazines, newspapers and the radio.

Global or international culture is rapidly expanding. Students should be able to find many examples from labels on trade store products to popular songs that come from overseas to the many personal items that they will have. This is also a good time for the teacher to discuss the differences between rural and urban people:

- Are urban people all becoming more culturally alike?
- Are rural people around the world more likely to maintain traditional parts of culture?
- Elaborations and integrating projects could follow up this type of discussion.

### When did culture start?

No one has any idea when culture started. This is a good discussion area for students. There is no correct answer. Culture may have started millions of years ago with the simple tools found with the remains of homo habilis and later with the more sophisticated tools of homo erectus. Did these very early humans sing and speak? Did they put flowers in their hair? No one has any idea. Or students can argue that human culture only started with modern homo sapiens. As a follow-up discussion, ask students where culture is taking us now? This is another theme that could be followed in an integrating project. It leads directly to change, globalisation and spreading cultures.

### The spread of cultures and globalisation

Papua New Guinea cultures along with all other cultures of the world are changing. There is no tribe of people left on Earth that is not impacted by changes from the cultures of the world. The greatest change is global warming and its impact on the world environment. Global warming is the direct result of culture and specifically of global technological culture for power and transport.

There are many other changes in communication, dress, transport and land use that are all a product of cultural mix and change today. One way for students to see this is to have them ask parents, grandparents and other relatives what their favourite music was when they were young, and then compare that with the favourite music of classmates today. This is one example of how different parts of different cultures are spreading and being adapted around the world.

Pages 85–92 in the Student Book cover the following themes. The table also includes sample questions and discussion points for use in the class and to set as study assignments. Students can research all these pictures (refer to the Picture Key on pages 143–144 of the Student Book) and find others to show that more people around the world are sharing ideas and beliefs. The table will also assist teachers with the section of the Student Book — Parts of culture around the world.

| Theme | Sample questions and discussion points |
|---|---|
| Arts (p85) | These pictures show two pieces of Latin American ornamentation that follow a mask theme along with an African mask and some samples of European art. They show how the human face is a recurring theme in art, from simple day-to-day objects to more complex expressions that include a sacred or religious element. Students could compare this art with the art of Papua New Guinea. Ask students:<br>– What do you think the purpose of these items is?<br>– How do they compare to the arts in Papua New Guinea?<br>– What makes them art?<br>– How do you know if something is art or not?<br>– What is the purpose of art?<br>– What are some of the other possible purposes of these objects? |
| Death (p86) | These pictures show an Irish graveyard (a traditional way of disposing of the dead in Europe) and a Balinese funeral procession. These pictures show how different cultures approach death. Both are expressions of cultures. Ask students:<br>– What do the ceremonies do for the dead and for the living?<br>– What are the different cultural attitudes to death? |

| Theme | Sample questions and discussion points |
|---|---|
| Religion (p86) | These pictures show a crowd of people waiting for a Buddhist monk to give them a blessing in Burma, a temple in Thailand, the interior of a Catholic church in Ecuador that is covered in gold gilding, and Laotian people holding prayers at a very old and sacred temple site. Ask students:<br>– Why should we respect people's religious beliefs?<br>– Why is religion so important in so many places?<br>– What type of cultural expressions of religion can we see in these pictures?<br>– What similarities can we see in the different cultures and pictures? What are the differences?<br>– What is the relationship between religion and art?<br>– How do these pictures compare with religious expression in Papua New Guinea? |
| Gender (p87) | These pictures include a Thai weaver. Weaving is a job for women in Thailand because it takes long hours and earns little money. (Note that before the Industrial Revolution, men were weavers in England and it was an important job that earned a good living.) There is a picture of a Latin American girl carrying kerosene to use at home. Again this is a type of 'women's work'. There are also pictures of some traditionally dressed Austrian villagers, and some young American boys with a cake that they are about to eat. The bigger boys are taking care of the little boy. Ask students:<br>– How does culture define roles by gender? (That is for boys and girls and for men and women?)<br>– How is this changing around the world?<br>– Why do you think that the girls and women often have to do the poor-paying or non-paying jobs?<br>– Who do you think baked the cake for the boys?<br>– How can you compare the roles you see in these pictures with roles for boys and girls, women and men in Papua New Guinea? |
| Family (p87) | These pictures show an extended settler family in the Amazon-Orinoco river catchments of South America, and a family in Southern Laos. The pictures show that families all over the world are recognisable and continue to practise special cultural traditions wherever they are. Ask students:<br>– What can you tell about the families from these pictures?<br>– What are different ways that families can express culture?<br>– Are there any pictures in these pages that do not apply to families and family activities?<br>– How do families strengthen cultures?<br>– How do families change cultures?<br>– What parts of Papua New Guinea culture does your family participate in?<br>– How does your family compare to the families in these pictures?<br>– What do you think is similar to your family?<br>– What do you think is different?<br>– How do you think you would fit into one of these families?<br>– What values do you think they have?<br>– What do you think is important to them in their culture? |

| Theme | Sample questions and discussion points |
|---|---|
| Education (p88) | These pictures show classroom scenes from Tibet and Colombia. Tibet is a colony of China and you can see the investment the Chinese government has made in having Tibetan students learn about Chinese culture. Colombia was a colony of Spain and the teaching language is Spanish – almost all indigenous languages are now lost. The Colombian class is much poorer. The investment is less. Ask students:<br>– How important is education to culture?<br>– What type of education are the students getting?<br>– How much can you tell about gender in each class? (Try to count the boys and girls.)<br>– How similar are the basics of primary education?<br>– Compare the pictures with your own classroom. |
| Language (p88) | These pictures show examples of Chinese, Greek, and American English. Ask students:<br>– What can you tell about language in these pictures?<br>– What cultural traits is the picture of American English showing?<br>– What are the main purposes of the Greek and Chinese signs in these pictures?<br>– What do the pictures tell us about global culture? |
| Pop culture (p89) | 'Pop' or popular culture is found around the world in many different expressions. The picture from inner Mongolia shows a typical advertisement for hair care and plastic flowers for sale. Inner Mongolia is in a cold dry place so plastic flowers are common. The other picture is a giant wooden statue of Paul Bunyan in Oregon, United States of America. He is a mythical figure from the early American timber industry. The story includes a huge blue ox that helped Paul chop down trees. There is a picture of an Australian fashion model. All the pictures cover different aspects of popular culture. The Paul Bunyan picture is also part of tourist culture. Often giant statues are put up to attract tourists to a place that may have little else to offer. Ask students:<br>– What do these pictures tell you about popular culture?<br>– How many different popular items can you find in the pictures?<br>– How do they compare with popular culture in Papua New Guinea?<br>– What can't the pictures show? (For example, songs and other parts of culture that are in a different medium.) |
| Sub-cultures (p89) | The pictures show various minority groups and can be used to stimulate discussions about what minorities contribute to the larger cultures of the world. Ask students:<br>– How important is it to keep some of the traditions of minority cultural groups?<br>– What can we learn from these groups?<br>– How are they part of the world's cultural heritage?<br>– How do these groups compare with traditional groups in Papua New Guinea? |
| Urban settlements (p90) | These pictures show views of Baltimore and San Francisco in the United States of America, and Hong Kong and London, England. Urbanisation is a growing feature of world culture. More than half the total population of the world now lives in cities. More people are migrating to urban settlements every day. Urban settlements have many modern cultural features like entertainment, transport, medical services, education and job opportunities. Urban settlements, like rural settlements, create different cultural landscapes. Urban settlements seem to be getting more and more similar. Students can discuss how cities are changing the cultures of the world. Ask students: |

| Theme | Sample questions and discussion points |
|---|---|
| Urban settlements (cont.) | – How do these cities compare with the cities of Papua New Guinea?<br>– How have Papua New Guinea cities been changing to become more like other cities of the world?<br>– What are cities doing to culture?<br>– Are cities helping global culture grow?<br>– Why do so many people want to come to cities?<br>– What differences can you see in the landscapes of the cities in the pictures? How do you explain the differences?<br>– What values can you see or determine about cities from these pictures?<br>– What seems important to city people? |
| Rural settlements (p90) | These pictures show rural settlements in Africa, on the Tonle Sap lake and river system of Cambodia and in the volcanic mountains of Flores Island, Indonesia. Students can find these places on a map. Rural settlements create very different cultural landscapes. Students can compare how people have adapted to these different environments. Students can also compare them with settlements in similar environments (lake, river or mountain areas) in Papua New Guinea. |
| Food (p91) | These pictures follow the retail market for food in different cultures. There is an Asian food stall, a South American trade store with food items, a Central American food market, and a meat market in Asia. There are many other aspects to food, such as producing it, preparing it and eating it. These areas offer other themes to follow in the culture of food. Students will be able to collect many different pictures of food and compare the food's place in different cultures or study it as part of global culture. They can look at food values, at food preparation and different ways of consumption. Ask students:<br>– How are foods viewed in different cultures?<br>– What important foods are shown in these pictures?<br>– How do you think people will prepare these foods?<br>– Where did these foods come from?<br>– How do these markets compare with Papua New Guinea?<br>– What sacred foods or sacred meals can you think of?<br>– How is food used in religion? |
| Shelter (p91) | These pictures show a house in Mexico, a Swiss mountain home, a traditional wealthy courtyard in a southern Chinese house and an Irish cottage. Ask students:<br>– What are the purposes of these houses?<br>– Why are they so different?<br>– How much of a house is really needed for shelter and how much expresses other things about the culture?<br>– How have these houses been adapted to the environment?<br>– What else do you think these houses are showing you about world cultures?<br>– How do they compare with houses in Papua New Guinea?<br>– What are the biggest differences? What are the similarities? |

| Theme | Sample questions and discussion points |
|---|---|
| Sports (p92) | These pictures show an American baseball game and a parade of athletes after the 2000 Sydney Olympic Games. There is no single global sport but there are a number of sports that bring many nations together. The Olympic Games bring athletes from around the world together every four years. It is an example of a growing global sharing of some aspects of sports culture. There are many other international sports associations, for example in soccer (football), cricket and tennis. Students can discuss how sport brings people from different cultures together and how it can divide them. Discussion can also focus on what values sports and sports people add to a culture. Ask students:<br>– How helpful are these values?<br>– Can some sporting values harm a society?<br>– How much has sport become part of international business?<br>– What is the purpose of sport in different cultures? |
| Work (p92) | These pictures show a Hong Kong job advertisement for domestic workers (maids) from Indonesia and the Philippines, a village enterprise for making and selling clay pots in Burma, fishermen in the South American Andes, Greek fishermen and African farmers. The discussion on work as a part of culture can be very wide-ranging. Economic activity (work) is fundamental to all cultures. Whether it is subsistence work or cash or paid employment, people must work to survive. Work can bring different cultures together. It can be rural or urban and it can be done very differently in different places. It has links to all the themes in this table. Students can discuss them all or elaborate on them. |

## Culture by continents

Another way of looking at different cultures around the world is to do it by studying each continent. The teacher will need to take care that students do not slip into stereotypes. Cultures are very complex and the Student Book is only able to cover some ideas very superficially.

### African cultures

Consider that Egypt is part of Africa and represents some 7000 years of culture and cultural influence. Today it is an Arab country that shares some cultural similarities with other parts of North Africa. And North Africa shares much with the Middle East, which is part of Asia. Much of Arab culture is adapted to very dry environments.

Southern African cultures are often represented as tribal although there are a number of examples of urban settlement in Southern Africa. One of the most noted features is music. Music brought by slaves to North and South America has led to the development of many different musical types that are now heard around the world: blues, jazz, soul, rock and roll, rap, hip-hop, tango, rumba, samba, mambo, bossa nova, salsa and reggae. For students who like music, there are any number of opportunities for integrating projects on the musical traditions that started with African cultures.

### European cultures

Students will see examples of items from European culture all around them. The printing press and printed books are just one example of the development of European culture. The Student Book is part of the European cultural heritage that developed modern printing and the worldwide distribution of books.

Many early civilisations developed systems of writing. There were different approaches to printing across the centuries. Many cultures developed some ideas and technologies that used some part of printing. For example:

- The Minoans who existed 4000 years ago, before the ancient Greek civilisation, had little blocks to print letters into soft clay.
- The Chinese still use stone rollers with symbols carved in them to ink messages on paper. This system is almost 2000 years old. You can still buy the rollers with special messages in the old part of Beijing city today.
- About 1400 years ago, the Chinese used wooden blocks for printing. And 1000 years ago, the Chinese invented another printing system using clay blocks held together with wax.
- Johannes Gutenberg, a German, is the father of modern printing. He invented a relatively simple printing process in the 1400s that was soon copied by others. This started the wider distribution of books. The first book was the Bible and the Gutenberg Bible is famous in European cultural history.
- Bibles, like other books, had to be hand-copied by scribes until the printing press arrived. More Bibles allowed more people to start reading them. This was the key to the development of the Protestant religions that changed much of the culture in many parts of Europe.

## Latin cultures

Latin cultures started with the ancient Romans. The Latin language provides the base for Italian, French, Spanish, Portuguese and Romanian. Many English words are derived from Latin, so English also has a major link to Latin heritage. Students with a dictionary can search for words that originally come from Latin. For example, decimal, per cent, legion, century, consul, lasso, politics.

South American cultures are often called Latin American cultures. This is because the Spanish and Portuguese who settled most of South America had a Latin-based language and culture. Latin America also includes Mexico, Central America and parts of the Caribbean islands. The Latin and Latin American cultures mix the Catholic religion with local traditions, cultural expressions and combinations of art. This is most clearly seen in the many cathedrals in both Latin Europe and Latin America. Other very visible or audible signs of Latin culture are colourful festivals, music, poetry and art.

## North American cultures

Today North American culture is dominated by the culture of the United States of America. Students will be able to find and analyse examples of this from many different sources. Secular cultural icons from the United States include Hollywood movies, democracy, fast food, music, and the invention of mass-produced automobiles for ordinary people (starting with the Ford motor company). There is also the spread of American religious culture through missionaries, radio programs and religious tracts. This has often been done in parallel with European culture.

## South American cultures

South America, Central America and Mexico are primarily all parts of Latin America. Since colonial times, these cultures have been greatly influenced by the Catholic Church. It is only in the last 20 to 30 years that evangelical

Protestantism has started to grow and change some aspects of culture in parts of South America. The dominant culture remains one of Latin and Catholic tradition mixed with indigenous art and belief systems. There are remnants of Inca, Maya, Chibcha and Aztec beliefs and art found in parts of Latin America today.

### Asian cultures

Like the other continents, Asia cannot really be reduced to a single cultural group. There is a minimum of five divisions and even these can vary:

- North Asia (Japan, China and Korea)
- Southeast Asia (the Philippines – with some Latin cultural items, Indonesia, Brunei, Malaysia, Vietnam, Burma, Laos and Thailand)
- The Indian subcontinent (India, Bangladesh and Pakistan)
- The Middle East is an Islamic cultural area (Yemen, Oman, Syria, Jordan, Lebanon, Israel, Saudi Arabia, Turkey, Iran, Iraq, Qatar, the Arab Emirates and Iran). It used to include India and Tibet but this has changed in modern times.
- Central Asia (part of western China, Mongolia, Kazakhstan, Uzbekistan and Afghanistan). Afghanistan can be counted as part of the Middle East.

### Australian cultures

Given the colonial history of Australia in Papua New Guinea, students will be able to find many examples of Australian cultural influences. It would be interesting if the teacher can find an Australian to speak on Australian culture. It has changed dramatically over the last 40 years. It is a much more international culture today with many distinct subcultures reflecting migration from places like Italy, Greece, the Pacific Islands, Asia and Africa. Aboriginal and Torres Strait Islanders have some of the oldest continuous culture in the world.

## Cultural icons

Another way students can study culture is through icons. An icon is an image or symbol. It represents some special part of the culture. This should be an easy concept for students to grasp and they will find many examples. It can also lead to discussion about cultural stereotypes. Sometimes icons can lead directly to stereotypes or other ways to belittle someone's culture.

## Melting pot or multiculturalism

How people treat culture is very important. There have been religious wars and other conflicts that use cultural differences to inspire hatred and violence. Nations have approached culture in different ways. Some have tried to keep their culture 'pure' whereas others have welcomed differences and explored change. Students can look at many different examples. Fundamentalist religions provide one area of possible study. These ideas also lead to questions about how to protect culture? Should anyone protect culture? Is change good or bad? There is a separate section in the Student Book that covers these ideas.

## Religion and language

Another way to look at culture around the world is through the spread of ideas. Religion and language are two different carriers of ideas. The teacher will need to take care in discussions about religion. The point to make is that the world needs to show tolerance and respect for different ideas, religions and different languages. There is no other way to peace. Freedom of religion is a human right. In some countries, the freedom to choose a language is a right; for example, French and English are both official languages in Vanuatu and Canada.

## Culture wars

Culture wars today refer to conflict between different belief systems. There are people who believe that women have a right to terminate their pregnancies. This conflicts with people who think that the unborn baby has a right to life no matter how small or unformed. There is a similar difference in thought about the right of same-sex couples to be married. These are contentious issues and the teacher must seek balance and respect in any discussion. These types of differences are found in many different religious groups from Christians, to Jews to Hindus to Muslims.

## Stereotypes

Stereotypes of different cultures are very common. They are insidious. Any examination immediately reveals that stereotypes cannot be true of a whole nation or group of people, and yet it is easy to slip into stereotyping. Papua New Guinea students will be familiar with this as there are many stereotypes about Papua New Guinea ethnic groups. (Highlanders, Sepiks, Islanders and so forth all have stereotypes of each other.) Students can seek out biased statements about cultures around the world. They can also look at how a government and its actions may not represent the culture or cultures of a country very well.

## The Internet

The Internet is a very powerful tool for spreading ideas, pictures, concepts and other cultural information. Some of the information on the Internet is very good. Some is totally false. Some is propaganda and some involves cruel exploitation of innocent people. No study of culture can avoid the impact of the Internet today and the changes that it may bring tomorrow. Some Papua New Guinea students will have access to the Internet and this should grow in the future.

## Cultural items

There are any number of cultural items from around the world that a student could choose as the base for a project. The Student Book gives a few examples, and there are many more for students to find from all over the world.

## Myths and legends

Myths and historical stories make up much of Papua New Guinea oral culture. There are many examples from other parts of the world and the Student Book covers some of them. Other examples include:

- Sour grapes from Aesop's Fables: Aesop was a slave in ancient Greece who told wise stories, called fables. He won his freedom as a result. In this story, a fox sees some grapes growing high off a wall. He tries to jump up to eat them but cannot reach, so he says, 'I didn't want them anyway because I am sure they are sour.' The fox is rationalising the situation, a common escape for many people.
- Santa Claus: this story is based on Saint Nicholas who secretly gave gifts to the poor and needy in medieval Europe.

- Pandora's box: this saying comes from an ancient Greek myth. Pandora was given a sealed box with all the disease and evils of the world in it. She was told not to open it, but decided to have a peek. As soon as she tried to look inside, all the evil escaped and she couldn't get it back in. 'Opening Pandora's box' is starting trouble that you cannot stop.
- A scapegoat: this saying comes from biblical times. People would choose a goat, tie bits of cloth with their sins recorded on them on to the goat, and then stone the goat to drive it and their sins away. Today, a scapegoat is anyone who unfairly takes the blame for something they didn't do.
- The Midas touch: this expression comes from another ancient Greek myth. King Midas was so greedy that he got his only wish that everything he touched turned to gold. Today, someone who has the Midas touch often means someone who is very lucky at making money. In fact, the point of the myth was that gold alone is not so valuable. Midas touched his daughter and she turned to gold, breaking his heart. The original myth had a more complex message about the evil of greed.
- A Benedict Arnold or a Quisling: these two expressions from history in two different cultures have the same meaning. These two men were both traitors to their country (Arnold betrayed the United States of America when it revolted against Britain and Quisling betrayed Norway to the Nazis during World War II.) To call someone a Quisling or a Benedict Arnold is to call them a traitor.
- Achilles heel: this saying comes from another ancient Greek myth. Achilles was a famous Greek warrior who was invincible because he had been dipped into a sacred river when he was a baby and this protected him from all weapons in battle. The only part of him that was unprotected was his heel, where he was held so as not to drown. When Achilles' enemies discovered this, they wounded him in the heel and this killed him. So an 'Achilles heel' is a weak point that can be attacked.
- Red herring: this saying from European fish markets has come to mean a worthless clue or a worthless piece of information when solving a problem. It is something that does not help you find the truth in an investigation.
- Sandwich: this piece of food was named for the Earl of Sandwich, in England around 1860. He was too busy playing cards to stop to eat so he put some meat between two pieces of bread and kept playing.
- A flash in the pan: this saying comes from the old musket pistols that had a pan with gunpowder in it to help ignite the charge. A misfire resulted in a flash in the pan but no bullet shot out of the musket pistol. A flash in the pan is something that can look dramatic but fails. If it refers directly to a person, it means that person is a failure or has failed.

## The Ancient Seven Wonders of the World

The Student Book gives a brief description of the seven wonders of the ancient world. The list is biased to Greek and Roman culture around the Mediterranean thousands of years ago. Other regions would have had different lists. The seven ancient wonders demonstrate how long tourists have been looking at special cultural sites. Doubtless, there were many before that as well. Ask students to think of what the seven wonders of traditional Papua New Guinea and the Pacific might have been. Integrating projects could consider models or posters of some of the ancient wonders.

## Destroying world culture

All parts of world culture are vulnerable to destruction. Wars have destroyed libraries and art galleries and other parts of culture with untold value. Time and natural hazards have also led to decay and destruction. There are still societies that actively seek to destroy cultural items in the name of religion, political systems or philosophies. Students will be able to find many examples of places at risk. Globalisation itself is a destroyer of some aspects of culture.

## Protecting the world's cultural heritage

There are many ways to protect culture. Books that record heritage items and other parts of culture, as well as many other mediums can help keep records even when parts of cultures are lost like language, songs or buildings. Museums and collectors can help protect the most valuable cultural items. The United Nations Educational, Scientific and Cultural Organisation (UNESCO) has a heritage list of over 800 special places based on culture or the environment.

- This chapter of the Student Book features a set of pictures on pages 109 to 116 that cover special cultural places or icons that have come to be recognised around the world as parts of different cultures. Students should find each place on a map and see what other information they can collect about these special expressions of culture around the world.

| | |
|---|---|
| Africa (p109) | Timbuktu is a traditional city in Africa, located in central Mali near the Niger River.<br><br>The Egyptian pyramids were tombs designed to protect the remains of Pharaohs to ensure they had eternal life. The Great Pyramid is located at Giza. |
| Asia (pp110–111) | Angkor Wat is the ruins of what was a temple and royal complex of the ancient Khmers. They had a powerful Buddhist kingdom located in Cambodia near Tonle Sap lake, from 900 to 1400.<br><br>The Taj Mahal was built in 1635 as a mausoleum (tomb) for a queen by her heartbroken husband. He was a Mogul (Islamic ruler) in India. The Moguls were a tolerant group of rulers who co-existed with Hindus.<br><br>The Great Wall of China extends over 3 000 kilometres. Building started before the birth of Jesus and continued for well over a 1 000 years. The wall failed to keep out invaders when the Chinese general in charge betrayed the emperor and let the enemy in.<br><br>The Potala Palace in Lhasa, Tibet, was the home of the Dalai Lama. He was the leader of the Tibetan people in a former theocratic state before Tibet was controlled by China. |
| Australia and the Pacific Islands (p112) | The Sydney Opera House has become a recent icon of Australia. It was only completed in the early 1970s.<br><br>The statues of Easter Island were made several hundred years ago as sacred protectors of different clans on the island. When crops and food ran out, the statues were vandalised by unhappy villagers. |
| Europe (pp113–114) | The Acropolis in Athens, Greece, reflects the golden age of ancient Greece from 478 to 404 BC (before the Christian age). The high point of Greek civilisation actually only lasted about 50 years.<br><br>The Eiffel Tower was created as a temporary structure for a world fair in 1889. The original idea was to tear it down, and this nearly happened. Instead, it was preserved and has become a famous French icon.<br><br>The Kremlin is the citadel in Moscow, Russia.<br><br>Stonehenge is a prehistoric site located on a plain in England. Its age is uncertain, but it is probably around 3 000 Years old. What actually happened there is also unknown. |
| North America (p115) | The Golden Gate Bridge, California, in the United States of America was the longest single span bridge in the world when it was completed.<br><br>Mayan ruins in southern Mexico and Guatemala reflect a complex early civilisation with a number system that included zero, hundreds of years before Europeans copied the zero concept from India. |
| South America (p116) | The statue of Christ Redeemer is in Rio de Janeiro, Brazil.<br><br>The Panama Canal is in Central America. |

# Integrating Projects

## About this strand

The Integrating Projects strand has one sub-strand, Societies and Communities. This strand provides students with an opportunity to apply a selection of everything they have learned to a project. Students can choose from any place in the world. The challenge will be to find information that is balanced.

There are two learning outcomes and these are applied jointly in the elaborations. The elaboration is the integrating project. A student should only be required to do one project and that can reflect aspects of one or both of the two learning outcomes. Students can present their projects to the class and in that way, share the learning outcomes so that everyone is exposed to both outcomes.

Some students may wish to look at international organisations. In many places, the information on these will be limited. The first part of the section on Teacher Information provides an outline of the United Nations and its principle affiliates. Students in some areas may be able to follow up on information about this organisation.

## 8.4.1 Using the social science process to describe another nation and propose ways for Papua New Guinea to contribute more to the region

## 8.4.2 Using the social science process to describe an international society and propose ways for Papua New Guinea to be more involved in international affairs

## Main ideas

There are many ways to study other nations of the world. Students can take any of the material covered in the text and apply it to a study of some aspect of another nation or some parts of another nation (or nations). The text covers world culture and world culture covers almost everything that human beings have done.

Students can look at history, trade items, sport, clothing, art, music, the environment or anything else that interests them. In this final project they should choose the area they wish to study. The role of the teacher is to be sure that there is information available for them and that they are interested in the topic. Remember, some students may change their minds as they go. It is important that they start this integrating project earlier rather than later in the school year.

The topics are almost infinite. Chapters 1 to 3 of the Student Book cover physical, environmental, government, political, social, economic, historical and cultural themes from around the world. Students may pursue any of these. The Student Book gives many examples of possible study areas.

Your task as teacher will be to ensure that students start their integrating project with plenty of time to do the initial studies. Be sure to schedule enough time for students to change their direction if they find they have taken a wrong step. The teacher will need to watch that projects stay simple enough for students to complete in the time available.

You may have some students work in groups if they can trust each other to do a fair share of work. It will be important to monitor the work to see that it gets done. Students can start gathering information early in the course. They may change their minds or narrow their field of interest as they go.

The final integrating project should have a minimum of two parts: a written report that is given to the teacher and an oral report that is presented to the class. Any of the following could be included in either the written or oral report:

- a set of posters about the topic
- a model that demonstrates the key parts of the topic
- a set of songs about the topic
- a series of maps and tables that explain the topic
- a game or role-play developed to explain the topic
- some other medium of expression suggested by the student or teacher.

The more students truly wish to follow a project the more they will learn. Listen to their suggestions. Encourage them to think about the world and what about it interests them. Remind them of the various sources of information they have available: newspapers, books, maps, radio, people in the community (which may include other teachers, visitors and travellers).

Students in urban areas will have more information resources – this may include access to television and the Internet. Teachers in rural areas can work with students to collect more information resources, like keeping newspapers for reference by everyone in the class. Rural teachers especially will need to think about how they can work with the class to build information resources for everyone to share.

## Example of elaborating a learning outcome on other places

**Strand:** Integrating projects

**Sub-strand:** Societies and Communities

**Focus:** Students choose an area of interest within the world for their final integrating project

**Learning outcomes:**

**8.4.1:** Students are able to use the social science process to describe another nation and propose ways for Papua New Guinea to contribute more to the region.

**8.4.2:** Students are able to use the social science process to describe an international society and to propose ways for Papua New Guinea to be more involved in international affairs.

Students may work in groups or individually. The key is to determine what each student is interested in and encourage work in that.

The curriculum allocates three hours a week to Social Science. This means that some portion of the project time will have to be done after class. It may also be possible to combine the project with another curriculum subject.

| Monday | Class days for 2 weeks | Friday |
|---|---|---|
| *Half-hour* | *10 minutes* | *10 minutes per student depending on class time* |
| Review the social science process: SEE-UNDERSTAND-ACT. Have students think about what they want to study. What will they see and what will they understand? Then have them consider how they will act. Will they produce a report? Do they want to produce a collection of pictures with an explanation or a story to explain what has happened? Do they want to produce a short report and then some type of cultural expression like an artefact, set of songs or some other product that is the result of their study? | Discuss the progress of projects with the different individuals or groups. Have students change or adapt their studies if they are having difficulties getting information. | Schedule oral reports with accompanying material over several class periods. Have a presentation on each integrated project. Allow enough time for the class to discuss the results. Based on the teacher and class comments on the presentation, allow the presenter two more days to make any final changes and turn in all material. Post the best material on the classroom walls if the location is secure. |

Alternative schedule: adapt to your particular timetable.

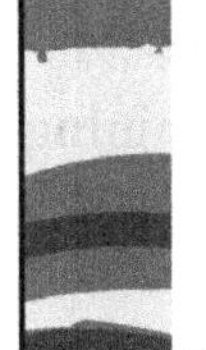

### Key words

United Nations, tourism, cities
(All other key words have been covered in the guide to the first three strands.)

**Possible assessment tasks**

It may be possible to start an integrating project while studying another strand. This will depend on the abilities of the class and the time available. It will depend very much on teacher initiative and class abilities.

Assessment could be based on three steps:

- SEE: evaluate how well the student has gathered information
- UNDERSTAND: evaluate how well the student has analysed and understood the information and come to a conclusion – is the conclusion logical?
- ACT: evaluate the final product – this will be oral and written material including posters, songs, models, games, role-play and/or other forms of expression.

Integrating projects are the last chance for students to apply the social science process at the end of three years of study. It should be a chance for them to choose a topic that interests them. For many, the difficulty will be access to information. Integrating projects, such as the following examples, should be a fun way to learn about the world. Remember that balance is the aim of all integrating projects. All the following material could be expanded into many formats including posters, role-plays, songs, models or any other medium of expression.

## Teacher information

### United Nations

The most comprehensive international organisation in terms of world coverage is the United Nations (UN). Students may see some UN activities at a local level and will find reference to different UN functions or groups in the news. There is a United Nations Development Programme office located in Port Moresby.

The UN started on 24 October 1945 when a group of nations signed the UN Charter. China, France, the Soviet Union, the United Kingdom and the United States of America were the key signatories. The original meeting to sign the Charter was held in San Francisco, in the United States of America. The United States donated land and funding to build a headquarters in New York City. Many countries now donate to the UN, although the United States remains the largest single donor.

The UN Charter sets out the UN's organisation and procedures, as well as the member states' rights and obligations. The Charter establishes the purposes of the UN:

'to maintain international peace and security; to develop friendly relations among nations; to co-operate in solving international economic, social, cultural and humanitarian problems and in promoting respect for human rights and fundamental freedoms; and to be a centre for harmonising the actions of nations in attaining these ends.'

The UN has six main parts:

- General Assembly
- Security Council
- Economic and Social Council

- Trusteeship Council
- International Court of Justice
- United Nations Secretariat.

There are other agencies, funds and programs linked to the UN. Two major ones are the UN Children's Fund (UNICEF) and the UN Development Programme (UNDP). There are another 15 autonomous specialised agencies linked to the UN, but acting within their own guidelines and reporting to their own governing bodies.

| ITU | International Telecommunication Union | Helps international cooperation for better telecommunications of all kinds. |
|---|---|---|
| UNESCO | UN Educational, Scientific and Cultural Organization | Promotes education for all, cultural development, protection of the world's natural and cultural heritage, international cooperation in science, press freedom and communication. |
| UNIDO | UN Industrial Development Organization | Promotes the industrial advancement of developing countries. |
| UPU | Universal Postal Union | Establishes international regulations for postal services, provides technical assistance and promotes cooperation in postal matters. |
| WHO | World Health Organization | Coordinates programs aimed at solving health problems and improving health for all people. (See example below.) |
| WIPO | World Intellectual Property Organization | Promotes international protection of intellectual property and fosters cooperation on copyrights, trademarks, industrial designs and patents. |
| WB | World Bank Group | Provides loans and technical assistance to developing countries to reduce poverty and advance sustainable economic growth. |
| WMO | World Meteorological Organization | Promotes scientific research on the Earth's atmosphere and climate change, and facilitates the global exchange of meteorological data. |
| WTO | World Tourism Organization | Serves as a global forum for tourism policy issues and a practical source of tourism know-how. |

Example: The WHO is one of the stronger UN agencies. It is working on its Eleventh General Program of Work. The title of this program is 'Engaging for health' and it is running from 2006 to 2015. This program approach to problems gives some idea of how the different agencies work. It is working on seven points to help improve world health:

- investing in health to reduce poverty
- building individual and global health security
- promoting universal coverage, gender equality and health-related human rights
- tackling the determinants of health
- strengthening health systems and equitable access
- harnessing knowledge, science and technology
- strengthening governance, leadership and accountability.

Students may be able to contact or view some WHO work locally. This is an example of what could be the start of an integrating project for those who are interested in the types of health problems the WHO tackles around the world.

## Tourism

The World Tourism Organisation is another UN affiliate. Tourism is an example of an area that has national and international parts. It has an impact on the environment, on social and economic organisation and on governments. Students could study tourism as an integrating project from many different angles. Here are a few ideas on the positive and negative aspects of tourism that could be used for a balanced study.

There are many economic benefits from tourism:

- It produces foreign exchange (money from countries overseas) and this helps government with balance of payment problems (money spent on goods imported into Papua New Guinea).
- It produces tax benefits for Papua New Guinea or another country where the tourists go. This means that government income increases and can be spent wisely on things like health and education.
- It creates employment. Tourism can make skilled and unskilled jobs available for people. Tourism can need a lot of people to make it work, so it can create many jobs.
- It can create a lot of growth in the economy by attracting the rich or many tourists.
- It diversifies the economy. You can have many different eggs in the economic basket and that is always better than just one (so for Papua New Guinea, for example, it would be coffee, tourism, copra and gold).
- It puts money into transport and other services that are good for the local people.
- It can help preserve or restore some cultural forms, traditional arts and handicrafts by providing a direct market for them.
- It can give money to help preserve the environment because this is the attraction for the tourists.
- It can help develop natural and or human-made areas for both tourists and local people to enjoy.
- It can help with the decentralisation of economic and commercial activities. Tourism can help develop areas that have nothing else but beauty or culture.
- It may require less time to develop than some other activities like planting new trees that take five years to bear fruit.

There are also problems with tourism:

- It can cause foreign exchange (money from countries overseas) to be lost to imports and repatriation of funds by foreign owners or partners.
- It can have high job creation and training costs with better jobs going to foreigners.
- It can result in high costs of infrastructure that can be aimed more to tourists than to locals.
- It can cost a country in incentives by granting tax deductions and tax holidays to a small group of local or overseas developers.
- It can result in an excessive dependence on foreign capital.
- It can result in foreign control and manipulation of the industry.
- It can result in inflation of local prices for goods and property.

- It can be an unstable market that is dependent on fashion, rumour, local stability and price.
- Investment can be hurt by competition from similar destinations.

Each problem or benefit can be further examined and argued in either direction. A similar list of benefits and problems can be developed for environmental and social issues. The following table gives four examples of the way this type of project could proceed. The history of tourism could then be compared with some other industry. In all cases there will be benefits and there will be problems. All the project can do is provide balance and a conclusion.

| Social benefits of tourism | Social problems with tourism |
|---|---|
| People come to understand different cultures and places, and international friendship improves. | Local people see rich tourists and become unhappy with their lives. They start to act like the tourists and behave wastefully. |
| Local people take more pride in their culture as they see how much tourists like it. | Tourism can become dependant on overseas knowledge and skills. |

| Environmental benefits of tourism | Environmental problems of tourism |
|---|---|
| Local people come to appreciate their own environments and places of natural beauty as they see how important they are for tourists. | So many tourists go to a place that the natural environment is damaged or destroyed. |
| People take better care of their local environment in expectation of tourism. | Strain is placed on infrastructure with increasing sewage and water usage impacting negatively on the environment. |

## Cities

Another example of an integrating project would be to compare one or two cities of the world with a Papua New Guinea city. For example, a student might be able to find articles and picture of New York or London or Beijing or Paris. They could compare this to a city they know, like Lae, Port Moresby, Wewak, Mt Hagen or Madang. Here are some study questions they might investigate for any project format:

- How big is the city?
- What is in it?
- How is it governed?
- What cultures can you find in these cities?
- How are the cities the same?
- How are the cities different?
- What resources are the cities using?
- How are the cities growing?
- What cultural icons do they have?
- How do the cultural icons compare with each other?

# Glossary

| | |
|---|---|
| **abolished** | stopped, made illegal |
| **advocates** | people or organisations that work for a particular cause |
| **arable** | land that is used for farming |
| **arms** | military weapons |
| **atheism** | a belief that there is no god |
| **atmosphere** | the gases that surround the Earth, including air |
| **atolls** | coral islands |
| **bias** | an opinion that comes from a particular direction or viewpoint |
| **candidate** | a person who stands for election |
| **caste** | a social class system based on birth |
| **circulation** | movement; the general circulation of the atmosphere is movement of winds around the Earth |
| **competition** | to compete for rewards; for example, businesses compete against each other for profits |
| **continental drift** | the movement of the continents through plate tectonics |
| **continental shelf** | the part of a continent that is under water where it meets the sea, sloping down to the deep ocean |
| **corrupt** | dishonest |
| **currents** | a large flow of water moving in a particular direction |
| **deciduous** | trees that lose their leaves in winter |
| **divine** | god-given, sacred |
| **duties** | an extra cost placed on imported trade goods (similar to tax) |
| **dynasties** | ruling families |
| **eligible** | suitable, with the right qualifications |
| **environment** | all of the physical things (whether natural or made by people) in a particular place |

| | |
|---|---|
| **evaporates** | when water heats up and turns into water vapour |
| **evergreen** | trees that keep their leaves all year round |
| **extinction** | when a particular species dies out |
| **finite** | limited |
| **fundamentalist** | extremely conservative |
| **globalisation** | the spread of culture, products and systems around the world; also a world economic system based on free trade |
| **global warming** | the heating up of the Earth's atmosphere |
| **globe** | a round shape; the Earth is often described as a globe |
| **greenhouse gases** | the gases that create global warming; carbon dioxide, methane and water vapour |
| **grid** | a series of lines that run parallel and perpendicular to each other |
| **hemispheres** | the two halves of the planet Earth; the Northern Hemisphere is above the Equator and the Southern Hemisphere is below it |
| **hereditary** | handed down through a family |
| **hieroglyphics** | a set of symbols used as an early form of writing |
| **humanity** | all the people on Earth |
| **hypothesis** | an idea or question upon which research can be based |
| **icons** | images or symbols of a culture |
| **indentured servants** | people who sell themselves into service for a fixed period of time |
| **infinite** | never-ending |
| **irrigation** | systems made by humans to bring water to food crops and animals often using trenches and canals |
| **latitude** | the location of a place north or south of the Equator |
| **longitude** | the location of a place east or west of the Prime Meridian |
| **magma** | molten rock |
| **mariners** | sailors |
| **market economy** | an economic system driven by supply and demand in free markets |
| **minority** | a small group, less than half |
| **monarchs** | leaders who are born into their position |
| **mummies** | preserved human bodies after death (some animals too) |

| | |
|---|---|
| **non-renewable** | finite or limited |
| **orbits** | moves around in a circular path |
| **patron** | sponsor or supporter |
| **population density** | the number of people living in a certain area, such as a square kilometre |
| **prehistory** | the period before recorded history |
| **precipitation** | rain, hail, sleet and snow |
| **predictions** | ideas about what will happen in the future |
| **preferences** | preferred choices |
| **prejudice** | an opinion formed without any reason or experience |
| **Prime Meridian** | a navigation line that runs from the North to South poles, through Greenwich, England |
| **protectorates** | small colonies or territories |
| **racism** | the belief that people are different depending on the colour of their skin or the country they belong to |
| **raw materials** | the basic goods used to create something; oil is a raw material that is used to make fuel |
| **regulations** | rules or laws made by a government |
| **rotates** | spins around in a circle on an axis |
| **sects** | small religious groups |
| **sphere** | a circular shape, like a globe |
| **status** | position in society |
| **stereotypes** | a biased view of a person from a particular place or culture |
| **stratosphere** | the outer layer of the atmosphere |
| **submerged** | underwater |
| **subsidies** | payments given by the government to help businesses (often given to farmers in Europe and the United States of America) |
| **surplus** | extra |
| **taxes** | money paid to the government by citizens |
| **tectonic plates** | the structures beneath the continents and oceans |
| **universe** | all of space to include our world, the sun, stars and beyond; also called the cosmos |